Bond

STRETCH
Verbal Reasoning
Tests and Papers

10–11+ years

Frances Down

Nelson Thornes

Published in 2012 by:
Nelson Thornes Ltd
Delta Place
27 Bath Road
CHELTENHAM
GL53 7TH
United Kingdom

12 13 14 15 16 / 10 9 8 7 6 5 4 3 2 1

A catalogue record for this book is available from the British Library

ISBN 978 1 4085 1866 3

Page make-up by GreenGate Publishing Services, Tonbridge, Kent

Printed and bound in Spain by GraphyCems

Introduction

What is Bond?

The Bond Stretch series is a new addition to the Bond range of Assessment papers, the number one series for the 11+, selective exams and general practice. Bond Stretch is carefully designed to challenge above and beyond the level provided in the regular Bond assessment range.

How does this book work?

The book contains two distinct sets of papers, along with full answers and a Progress Chart:

- Focus tests, accompanied by advice and directions, which are focused on particular (and age-appropriate) Verbal Reasoning question types encountered in the 11+ and other exams, but devised at a higher level than the standard Assessment papers. Each Focus test is designed to help raise a child's skills in the question type as well as offer plenty of practice for the necessary techniques.

- Mixed tests, which are full-length tests containing a full range of Verbal Reasoning question types. These are designed to provide rigorous practice, perhaps against the clock, for children working at a level higher than that required to pass the 11+ and other Verbal Reasoning tests.

- Full answers are provided for both types of test in the middle of the book.

- At the back of the book, there is a Progress Chart which allows you to track your child's progress.

How much time should the tests take?

The tests are for practice and to reinforce learning, and you may wish to test exam techniques and working to a set time limit. We would recommend your child spends 50 minutes to answer the 85 questions in each Mixed paper. You can reduce the suggested time by five minutes to practise working at speed.

Using the Progress Chart

The Progress Chart can be used to track Focus test and Mixed paper results over time to monitor how well your child is doing and identify any repeated problems in tackling the different question types.

Focus test 1 — Similars and opposites

Always read this type of question carefully, as most of them will have similar <u>and</u> opposite options.

Underline the pair of words which are the most similar in meaning.

Example   come, go   <u>roams, wanders</u>   fear, fare

More than one set of the answers may apply. Look for the most appropriate.

1	rush, hurry	brighten, dawn	celebrate, perform
2	greed, hunger	number, numeral	below, above
3	cat, mouse	dog, wolf	bear, pig
4	how, why	in, on	by, near
5	hard, tough	rough, smooth	flimsy, rigid
6	aunt, grandchild	niece, father	brother, sister

6

Find the word that is opposite in meaning to the word in capital letters and that rhymes with the second word.

Example   SHARP   front   <u>blunt</u>

7	LOWER	graze	_____
8	LOVE	wait	_____
9	POLITE	food	_____
10	SLOW	flick	_____
11	IMMENSE	cute	_____
12	LIE	youth	_____

If you cannot find a suitable opposite word, try experimenting with rhyming words.

6

Underline the one word in the brackets which will go equally well with each of the words outside the brackets.

Example   word, paragraph, sentence   (pen, cap, <u>letter</u>, top, stop)

13 pillow, blanket, duvet   (night, bed, bedroom, rug)

14 pink, brown, yellow   (crayons, rainbow, paint, grey)

15 Birmingham, Cardiff, Belfast   (England, Leeds, Paris, Europe)

16 oak, ash, willow   (cricket, shrub, beech, country)

17 page, chapter, index   (writer, contents, capital, pencil)

18 traffic, bedside, moon   (car, street, room, light)   ( ) 6

Underline the two words, one from each group, which are the most opposite in meaning.

Example   (dawn, <u>early</u>, wake)   (<u>late</u>, stop, sunrise)

19 (brave, shy, ask)   (deny, hero, timid)

20 (rise, up, climb)   (high, low, down)

21 (rainy, dry, sunny)   (wet, cloudy, icy)

22 (twin, match, similar)   (opposite, same, alike)

23 (crying, laugh, happy)   (smiling, sad, joy)

24 (find, hide, seek)   (win, lose, loose)   ( ) 6

> **Remember: opposites not similar.**

Underline the one word in the brackets which will go with the word outside the brackets in the same way as the first two words go together.

Example   good, better   bad, (naughty, worst, <u>worse</u>, nasty)

25 tired, sleepy   awake, (daytime, alert, bed, up)

26 even, odd   level, (flat, peculiar, floor, sloping)

27 mystery, solve   task, (perform, relax, brain, reach)

28 board, cup   cause, (saucer, plank, be, reason)

29 large, vast   jog, (run, crawl, sprint, trot)

30 stripe, strip   peace, (calm, part, take, pace)   ( ) 6

> **Make sure you match the second pair of words in the same way as the first.**

Focus test 2 Sorting words

Underline the one word in the brackets which will go equally well with both the pairs of words outside the brackets.

Example rush, attack   cost, fee   (price, hasten, strike, <u>charge</u>, money)

> Take care. Often each word in the brackets will go well with one lot of words. Look for one that goes well with both.

1 command, control law, guideline (measure, rule, govern, call, lead)

2 timepiece, clock observe, monitor (time, look, pay attention, regard, watch)

3 cut, trim slap, smack (clip, prune, strike, slice, cuff)

4 pale, not dark gentle, soft (faint, delicate, flimsy, light, bright)

5 adorable, charming sugary, honeyed (cute, lovable, sweet, pleasant, fine)

6 movement, flow modern, present (push, now, river, current, run)

6

Find the three-letter word which can be added to the letters in capitals to make a new word. The new word will complete the sentence sensibly.

Example The cat sprang onto the MO. <u>USE</u>

> For these questions, use the sense of the sentence to help you make a sensible guess.

7 I will RY your books for you if your arm is too sore. _____

8 You must drink lots of WR every day to stay healthy. _____

9 The fairy GODMOR helped Cinderella to go to the ball. _____

10 Pat has lots of goldfish in his GAR pond. _____

11 Little Monica is too NG to learn to tie her shoelaces. _____

12 All the cars, lorries and BS drove more slowly in the heavy rain.

_____

6

Rearrange the muddled words in capital letters so that each sentence makes sense.

Example There are sixty SNODCES <u>seconds</u> in a UTMINE <u>minute</u>.

13 Use the BZRAE _____ crossing to FESLAY _____
cross the road.

14 The CCIRKTE _____ match was stopped as it REPODU
_____ with rain.

15 The High ETSRET _____ shops were full of sale GRABNSAI
_____.

16 The RNHCABSE _____ of the trees were GNIMVO
_____ in the wind.

17 The train PPESTOD _____ at the ATSIONT _____
for a long time.

18 The circus clowns made NEERVOEY _____ HGULA
_____.

6

Underline two words, one from each group, that go together to form a new
word. The word in the first group always comes first.

Example (hand, <u>green</u>, for) (light, <u>house</u>, sure)

19 (in, post, hill)   (stance, stamp, steep)

20 (thin, fat, part)   (nor, her, nets)

21 (up, ape, can)   (pear, start, down)

22 (came, son, high)   (light, down, lives)

23 (an, in, to)   (grey, gather, other)

24 (off, of, on)   (sit, put, ten)

> Take one word at
> a time from the
> left bracket and
> put it in front of
> each of the right
> bracket words.

6

Find a word that can be put either in front or at the end of each of the
following words to make new, compound words.

Example cast   fall   ward   pour   <u>down</u>

25 right   load   roar   stairs   _____

26 corn   gun   pet   per   _____

27 stream   bath   shot   thirsty   _____

28 knock   black   wash   blow   _____

29 false   brother   child   mother   _____

30 out   lamp   hole   pipe   _____

6

Focus test 3 Selecting letters

Which one letter can be added to the front of all of these words to make new words?

> Experiment with putting various letters in front of each of the words until you hit on the correct one.

Example <u>c</u>are   <u>c</u>at   <u>c</u>rate   <u>c</u>all

  1 __ear   __row   __rip   __lad

  2 __utter   __read   __east   __ladder

  3 __ridge   __ear   __our   __lower

  4 __bout   __board   __round   __tone

  5 __lever   __able   __oast   __rate   **5**

Find the letter that will end the first word and start the second word.

Example drow (<u>n</u>) ought

  6 ho (__) ater   8 bette (__) ose

  7 gree (__) ever   9 danc (__) ver   **4**

> Look at the word on the left and find various letters that could finish that word. Then see which one you can use to start the word on the right.

Find the two letters that will end the first word and start the second word.

Example pas (<u>ta</u>) ste

  10 becau (__ __) at   12 traff (__ __) icle

  11 ga (__ __) ner   13 chur (__ __) icken   **4**

Find the letter which will complete both pairs of words, ending the first word and starting the second. The same letter must be used for both pairs of words.

Example mea (<u>t</u>) able   fi (<u>t</u>) ub

  14 carro (__) iger   burn (__) ry

15 gre (__) ellow   tr (__) et

16 cur (__) est   or (__) end

17 stic (__) nit   struc (__) ing

If you don't succeed with one pair, look at the other.

○ 4

Move one letter from the first word and add it to the second word to make two new words.

Example	hunt	sip	<u>hut</u>	<u>snip</u>
18	plane	last	_____	_____
19	drift	hear	_____	_____
20	treason	seam	_____	_____
21	platter	pear	_____	_____
22	freight	fed	_____	_____

○ 5

Add one letter to the word in capital letters to make a new word. The meaning of the new word is given in the clue.

Example PLAN   simple   <u>plain</u>

23 HARD   listened   _____

24 BITER   sour   _____

25 SUCK   glued   _____

26 BOAT   brag   _____

Keep an eye on the meaning to help you.

○ 4

Remove one letter from the word in capital letters to leave a new word. The meaning of the new word is given in the clue.

Example AUNT an insect <u>ant</u>

Approach this in the same way as above but take a letter away rather than add one.

27 PLOTTER   clay worker   _____

28 DANGER   fury   _____

29 PRICKLE   chutney   _____

30 WARY   droll   _____

○ 4

Finding words

Underline the two words which are the odd ones out in the following groups of words.

Example black <u>king</u> purple green <u>house</u>

> Three of the words have something in common. Look for the link. Above, it is colours.

1 suitcase	bag	crayon	ornament	rucksack
2 minute	clock	small	tiny	watch
3 lion	giraffe	bear	leopard	tiger
4 go	stay	leave	remain	depart
5 consider	ponder	think	educate	exercise
6 battle	engine	elephant	bath	brilliance

6

Change the first word of the third pair in the same way as the other pairs to give a new word.

Example bind, hind   bare, hare   but, <u>hut</u>

7 climb, limb	plate, late	drain, _____
8 boat, beat	moan, mean	load, _____
9 said, aids	shear, hears	slime, _____
10 card, dark	leap, peak	fool, _____
11 plea, leap	near, earn	mite, _____
12 sold, sale	moth, mate	pony, _____

6

Underline the one word in each group which **cannot be made** from the letters of the word in capital letters.

Example STATIONERY   stone   tyres   ration   <u>nation</u>   noisy

13 CHARACTER	tracer	carer	chart	church	cheat
14 BREAKING	baking	grain	banker	brink	engine
15 PLASTERER	plates	treats	please	pester	repast

3

Underline the one word in each group which **can be made** from the letters of the word in capital letters.

Example CHAMPION camping notch peach cramp <u>chimp</u>

16 WANDERING dangers dawning raining drawer window

17 DRAGONFLY lagoon grandly found larder fondle

18 TROMBONE noble broth number broom tremor (3

Underline the two words in each line which are made from the same letters.

Example TAP PET <u>TEA</u> POT <u>EAT</u>

> Scan the words quickly and see if a pair jumps out. If you don't see the answer, look through word by word at individual letters.

19 DUSTY DIRTY RADIO RODEO STUDY

20 BLASTS STABLE BLADES BLEATS LABELS

21 TOWELS STROLL LOWEST SWELLS TEASEL

22 PRICES PRINCE PRIEST CENTRE STRIPE

23 STORES SOREST TRUSTS STROKE STRAIT

24 TREATS LEARNT STEERS TRAILS ANTLER (6

Find the four-letter word hidden in each sentence. Each begins at the end of one word and ends at the beginning of another word, and can cover two or three words. The order of the letters may not be changed.

Example We had bat<u>s and</u> balls. <u>sand</u>

> Scan quickly to see if you can spot the answer. Check the vowels. Then work through the sentence, word by word.

25 I saw her as I was walking down the road. _____

26 As I am tall, I can reach every book on the shelf. _____

27 Today the weather is cold for the time of year. _____

28 Mudit's hands were cold as he had forgotten his gloves. _____

29 Do not forget that the mayor is coming to school tomorrow.

_____

30 Mondays are my worst days of the week in term time. _____ (6

Look at the first group of three words. The word in the middle has been made from the two other words. Complete the second group of three words in the same way, making a new word in the middle.

Example PA<u>IN</u>   INTO   <u>T</u>OOK   ALSO   <u>SOON</u>   ONLY

> Look carefully at the first set of three words. Sometimes the pattern is straightforward, as in these:

#						
1	CARE	RENT	WANT	FIRE	_____	MOST
2	PAID	PATH	THIN	STEM	_____	OPAL
3	BARE	CARE	COMB	TIME	_____	MAUL
4	ICED	WISH	WASH	OPEN	_____	BATH
5	LIFE	TAIL	ATOM	DISH	_____	ARCH

5

> Sometimes, letters have to be worked out individually or there are several options with repeat letters:

#						
6	PAIN	PANE	ENDS	CROP	_____	WORK
7	BALL	BABY	BUOY	TIME	_____	SUNS
8	DRAW	WIND	WINK	MUFF	_____	GROW
9	POLE	LATE	TALL	KIND	_____	RACE
10	BOAT	COMB	COME	KNIT	_____	PEAR
11	TREE	BEAT	BOAT	EVIL	_____	MUCH
12	BOAT	ATOM	MATE	FATE	_____	RUSK
13	TOAD	COAT	ACTS	TINY	_____	SPIN
14	EACH	AREA	ARCH	ANTS	_____	BEAK
15	LEAF	FOIL	LION	LASH	_____	DRUM

10

Change the first word into the last word, by changing one letter at a time and making a new, different word in the middle.

Example CASE   <u>CASH</u>   LASH

16 CRAB   _____   GRUB

17 PRIM   _____   PRAY

18 SAKE   _____   BIKE

19 CAGE   _____   BAKE

20 FIRM   _____   TIRE

> Write down the letters that remain the same. Substitute the remaining letters one at a time.

5

Change the first word into the last word, by changing one letter at a time and making two new, different words in the middle.

> Do these in the same way. Work out which letter needs to be replaced first to make a word to lead to the next missing word.

Example CASE   <u>CASH</u>   <u>WASH</u>   WISH

21 WICK   _____   _____   SUCH

22 ROAD   _____   _____   LARD

23 WIDE   _____   _____   FIRM

24 SOFT   _____   _____   LOUD

25 BOOK   _____   _____   LUCK

26 TALL   _____   _____   TOAD

27 DRIP   _____   _____   TRAY

28 COOL   _____   _____   FOUR

29 LANE   _____   _____   FIND

30 FULL   _____   _____   FAIR

10

Now go to the Progress Chart to record your score!   Total **30**

Focus test 6 Substitution and logic

If A = 6, B = 3, C = 11, D = 5 and E = 2, what are the values of these calculations? Write each answer as a number.

> Replace the letters with numbers and work out the calculations.

1 C − (A + B) = _____

4 (D + E + A) − C = _____

2 D^2 − C = _____

5 $\dfrac{(C + D)}{E}$ = _____

3 EA ÷ B = _____

 5

Using the same values, what are the values of these calculations? Write each answer as a letter.

6 (A + C) − DB = _____

7 (C + D) − DE = _____

> Do exactly the same but turn the number answer into its letter value.

2

If T = 4, B = 7, R = 3, A = 1, D = 5 and O = 2, find the sum of these words when the letters are added together.

8 BOAT _____   **9** TOAD _____   **10** ROOT _____

3

Read the first two statements and then underline one of the four options below that must be true.

> More than one statement may be true, but you must look for the only one that has to be true, given the information.

11 'Maya loves going on holiday. This year she is going to Greece.'

    A Last year Maya went to France.

    B Maya likes Greece best.

    C Maya is going to Greece.

    D Greece is a popular place to go on holiday.

12 'Beetles are a type of insect. Insects have six legs.'

    A All animals are insects.

    B Beetles are small.

    C Animals have six legs.

    D Beetles have six legs.

2

In a test at school out of a total of 40 marks, Jo got half of them right. Kate got only 14 out of 40, while Tina only made seven mistakes. Anya made 11 mistakes and Dhruv got five more right than Jo.

Before you answer, write down the marks each child received.

13 Who got the most marks? _____

14 Who got less than Dhruv but more than Kate? _____

15 Who got 4 more marks than Dhruv? _____   ◯ 3

In French, Adrian sat somewhere to the left of Jasmine who sat somewhere to the left of Robert. Saskia and Jasmine did not sit next to each other. Connor sat next to Mo but not Robert. Mo sat somewhere to the right of Jasmine.

1	2	3	Robert	4	5

LEFT   RIGHT

Write a list of the children's names. Then write down their possible places beside the names as you read through sentence by sentence and eliminate the places as you progress.

Where did each child sit?

16 Adrian _____   17 Jasmine _____   18 Saskia _____

19 Connor _____   20 Mo   _____   ◯ 5

SWANSEA   SPALDING   SOUTHAMPTON   SOLIHULL   STOCKPORT
If these towns are put into alphabetical order, which comes:

21 first? _____   22 last? _____   23 fourth? _____   ◯ 3

If the days of the week are put into alphabetical order, which comes:

24 first? _____   25 last? _____

26 the one before Saturday?   _____

27 in the middle?   _____   ◯ 4

If the letters of the word BREAKING are written alphabetically, which comes:

28 first? _____   29 fourth? _____   30 seventh? _____   ◯ 3

Now go to the Progress Chart to record your score!   Total ◯ 30

Focus test 7   Codes

First line up the code with the word:

G R A T E F U L

5 8 7 3 9 2 1 6

Then substitute the letters for numbers.

If the code for GRATEFUL is 5 8 7 3 9 2 1 6.
Encode each of these words using the same codes.

1 GATE _____   **2** FURL _____

Decode these words using the same code as above.

3 3 9 7 8 _____   **4** 3 8 1 9 _____

5 If the code for SHEPHERD is K T O N T O Z L, what is the code for DRESS? _____

6 Using the same code, what does K N O O L stand for? _____

7 If the code for TOMORROW is ↑ ← → ← ↓ ↓ ← ↙, what is the code for WORM? _____

8 Using the same code, what does ↓ ← ← ↑ stand for? _____

9 If the code for FOUNTAIN is c X 9 P 8 e @ P, what does P X 9 P stand for? _____

10 Using the same code, what is the code for INTO? _____   ⟩10

Match the right word to each code given below.

REED   BARE   BEAR   BARB

11 x v w z   _____

12 x w z x   _____

13 z v v y   _____

14 x w z v   _____

> Look for some letters that stand out. In this case, all the words begin with B except one and REED also has double E.

15 Using the same code, what does z v w y stand for? _____   ⟩5

Solve the problems by working out the letter code. The alphabet has been written out the help you.

A B C D E F G H I J K L M N O P Q R S T U V W X Y Z

Example   If the code for CAT is D B U, what is the code for DOG? <u>E P H</u>

16 If the code for TABLE is V C D N G, what is the code for CHAIR?

_____

17 If the code for PAPER is Q B Q F S, what does C P P L T mean?

_____

18 If the code for HEDGE is F C B E C, what is the code for TREES? _____

19 If the code for SHELF is O D A H B, what does C N E H H mean? _____

Look at the relationship between each of the letters and its code.

○ 4

Example If the code for CAB is 3 1 2, what is the code for EGG? <u>5 7 7</u>

> Is there a link in the numbers? A is the first letter, C is the third.

20 If the code for DEAF is 4 5 1 6, what is the code for HIGH? _____

21 If the code for CHAFF is 3 8 1 6 6, what does 1 2 9 4 5 stand for? _____

○ 2

Example If the code for PEACH is O F Z D G, what is the code for APPLE? <u>Z Q O M D</u>

> This time the pattern alternates, letter by letter. If two letters in a word are the same, they are not necessarily the same code letter.

22 If the code for DRESS is E Q F R T, what is the code for SHIRT? _____

23 If the code for TREBLE is V Q G A N D, what is the code for VOICE? _____

Think of the alphabet as a continuous line, so YZ leads to AB etc.

24 If the code for STYLE is Q U W M C, what does T P E V C stand for? _____

25 If the code for MATHS is N B S G T, what does U J L D T stand for? _____

26 If the code for TIGER is U H H D S, what is the code for ZEBRA? _____

27 If the code for LAUGH is J Y S E F, what does F Y N N W stand for? _____

28 If the code for SORRY is R Q Q T X, what is the code for TEARS? _____

29 If the code for WATER is A Z X D V, what does Z Z P T I stand for? _____

30 If the code for DIVE is C G S A, what is the code for BEAD? _____

○ 9

Now go to the Progress Chart to record your score! Total ○ 30

Focus test 8 Sequences

Complete the following sentences in the best way by underlining one word from each set of brackets.

Example Tall is to (tree, <u>short</u>, colour) as narrow is to (thin, white, <u>wide</u>).

> Look for the relationship between the pairs of statements. The second pairing must be completed in the same way.

1 Snow is to (white, flake, cold) as sun is to (day, world, hot).

2 Dog is to (bark, pet, bone) as (person, cat, mouth) is to speak.

3 Diamond is to (necklace, heart, jewel) as (giant, spade, sports) is to club.

4 (Owl, Other, Clever) is to wise as dense is to (think, thin, thick).

4

Find the missing letters. The alphabet has been written out to help you.

A B C D E F G H I J K L M N O P Q R S T U V W X Y Z

> Do these in the same way. Look for the pattern. Use the alphabet line to help you.

Example AB is to CD as PQ is to <u>RS</u>.

5 FG is to JK as PQ is to _____.

6 ZY is to YX as ON is to _____.

7 MK is to IG as EC is to _____.

8 AP is to BQ as CR is to _____.

9 HL is to JJ as RV is to _____.

10 Ta is to Ya as Za is to _____.

11 AZ is to BY as CX is to _____.

12 UN is to WP as YR is to _____.

8

> Most of the time in these sequences, the letters work independently, like these.

Find the two missing pairs of letters in the following sequences. The alphabet has been written out to help you.

A B C D E F G H I J K L M N O P Q R S T U V W X Y Z

Example CQ   DP   EQ   FP   <u>GQ</u>   <u>HP</u>

There are two ways of tackling these sequences. Check to see if the letters are working together (as below) or independently as on the previous page.

13 AB   DE   GH   JK   ___   ___

14 ___   XW   VU   TS   ___   PO

15 RS   VW   ___   DE   ___   LM

16 JH   FD   ___   ___   TR   PN

17 MA   NC   ME   ___   MI   ___

18 GV   ___   CV   AW   ___   WW

19 AK   DI   GG   JE   ___   ___

20 ___   XG   VH   ___   RJ   PK

21 CHu   Plv   CJw   ___   ___   PMz

> Look at the letters separately with these ones.

⑨

Find the two missing numbers in the following sequences.

Example 2 4 6 8 <u>10</u> <u>12</u>

22 23 25 ___ 29 ___ 33

23 16 ___ 10 ___ 4 1

24 ___ 30 25 20 15 ___

25 2 ___ 8 ___ 32 64

26 18 17 15 12 ___ ___

27 ___ ___ 19 22 24 25

28 20 ___ 25 9 30 6 ___ 3

29 6 4 6 6 ___ ___ 6 10

30 17 ___ 14 9 ___ 10 8 11

> Look for the pattern between the numbers.

> Sometimes, in these questions, the increase/decrease is irregular.

> Check for numbers going up and down. If this is the case, look at alternate numbers.

⑨

Now go to the Progress Chart to record your score!   Total   ㉚

Mixed paper 1

Underline the pair of words which are the most similar in meaning.

Example come, go   <u>roams, wanders</u>   fear, fare

1 top, bottom   glide, soar   leaf, fruit

2 prick, pierce   needle, thread   sew, mend

3 combine, alter   crowd, throng   run, hide

4 pick, mix   stir, sleep   select, choose

5 fix, break   needy, rich   poor, unfortunate

5

Find the three-letter word which can be added to the letters in capitals to make a new word. The new word will complete the sentence sensibly.

Example The cat sprang onto the MO. <u>USE</u>

6 Dad put the tools back into the garden D. _____

7 "Ready, SDY, go!" shouted the starter at Sports Day. _____

8 The puddles were so deep, I got my socks and SS wet.

_____

9 I felt guilty because I GOT my friend's birthday. _____

10 We studied the Tudors in TORY lessons. _____

5

Which one letter can be added to the front of all of these words to make new words?

Example <u>c</u>are   <u>c</u>at   <u>c</u>rate   <u>c</u>all

11 __pine   __hut   __lit   __will

12 __lag   __arming   __light   __ill

13 __ear   __hinge   __rite   __on

14 __at   __aster   __we   __vent

15 __ink   __otter   __eel   __udder

5

Underline the two words which are the odd ones out in the following groups of words.

Example	black	king	purple	green	house
16	stone	rock	chalk	hill	mountain
17	basin	tap	bath	map	sink
18	right	left	wrong	correct	accurate
19	under	beneath	below	on	inside
20	Mediterranean	Atlantic	Pacific	Indian	North

5

Look at the first group of three words. The word in the middle has been made from the two other words. Complete the second group of three words in the same way, making a new word in the middle.

Example	PAIN	INTO	TOOK	ALSO	SOON	ONLY
21	JUMP	JUST	MOST	DOOR	_____	PIGS
22	BRIM	BITE	FATE	SLIP	_____	GONG
23	COIN	INTO	TOMB	BAKE	_____	EPIC
24	ZIPS	SPIN	CORN	BINS	_____	JEEP
25	STUD	DUST	STOP	GLUM	_____	USED

5

If a = 4, b = 2, c = 7, d = 3 and e = 5, work out the values of these calculations.

26 $(a + b + c) - (d + e)$ = _____

27 $ae - b$ = _____

28 $(e + c) \div a$ = _____

29 $d^2 - b^2$ = _____

30 $(c - a) + (d - b)$ = _____

5

If the code for SHOPPING is 7 6 1 3 3 5 2 4, what are the codes for the following words?

31 PINS _____

33 GOSSIP _____

32 SING _____

3

Using the same code, what do the following codes stand for?

34 6 1 3 5 2 4 _____

35 6 5 4 6 _____

2

Complete the following sentences in the best way by choosing one word from each set of brackets.

Example Tall is to (tree, <u>short</u>, colour) as narrow is to (thin, white, <u>wide</u>).

36 Window is to (glass, view, curtain) as (tree, door, fire) is to wood.

37 Hill is to (mountain, high, cold) as valley is to (river, low, steep).

38 Foal is to (horse, young, race) as lamb is to (kebab, sheep, field).

39 Kettle is to (kitchen, boil, water) as (hot, wash, bath) is to bathroom.

40 (Toe, Shin, Foot) is to leg as finger is to (hand, arm, nail).

5

Add one letter to the word in capital letters to make a new word. The meaning of the new word is given in the clue.

Example PLAN   simple   <u>plain</u>

41 RIGHT   a scare   _____

42 SPOT   game   _____

43 BEAR   facial hair   _____

44 PEAT   fold   _____

45 CAVE   cut, slice   _____

5

Underline two words, one from each group, that go together to form a new word. The word in the first group always comes first.

Example (hand, <u>green</u>, for)   (light, <u>house</u>, sure)

46 (cub, surf, live)   (bend, board, belt)

47 (white, water, green)   (home, proof, cloud)

48 (back, from, sum)   (wood, were, ward)

49 (be, in, on)   (gun, end, sett)

50 (cap, free, card)   (land, oil, able)

5

Change the first word into the last word, by changing one letter at a time and making a new, different word in the middle.

Example CASE   <u>CASH</u>   LASH

51 FARM   _____   HARK

52 SNUB   _____   SNAG

53 LIKE   _____   WIFE

54 SNOW   _____   GLOW

55 MANE   _____   MUTE   **5**

In a sports shop, different types of balls were placed in a row of containers. From the information, work out where each type of balls were.

A	B	TABLE TENNIS	C	D	E

The tennis balls were at one end of the display.

The rugby balls and hockey balls were next to each other.

The cricket balls were next to the table tennis balls and the hockey balls.

The footballs were in the spare place.

56 A = _____   **59** D = _____

57 B = _____   **60** E = _____

58 C = _____   **5**

Find the word that is opposite in meaning to the word in capital letters and that rhymes with the second word.

Example   SHARP   front   <u>blunt</u>

61 CLEAR   paint   _____

62 KIND   stool   _____

63 SANE   glad   _____

64 TIMID   slave   _____

65 ADORE   wait   _____   **5**

Find the letter that will end the first word and start the second word.

Example   drow (<u>n</u>) ought

66 dat (___) very   **69** spil (___) iver

67 jaz (___) ebra   **70** stuf (___) rog

68 brea (___) ite   **5**

Underline the one word in each group which **cannot be made** from the letters of the word in capital letters.

Example STATIONERY   stone   tyres   ration   <u>nation</u>   noisy

71 DISTANCE   stand   dance   stain   caned   nasty

72 STARVING   grand   grants   strain   saving   string

73 SQUEALED   sealed   duels   ladles   deals   eased

74 TRUNCHEON   trench   torch   chant   tenor   thorn

75 SPURTING   spurn   trump   grins   spring   grunts   **5**

If the code for GARDEN is * @ ? # $ ~, what do the following codes stand for?

76 # ? @ *   _____   79 * ? $ $ ~   _____

77 ? @ ~ *   _____   80 * ? @ # $ _____

78 ~ $ @ ?   _____   **5**

Find the two missing numbers in the following sequences.

Example   2 4 6 8 <u>10</u> <u>12</u>

81   7   17   __   37   __   57

82   __   __   8   16   32   64

83   33   __   27   24   21   __

84   3   4   6   __   13   __

85   40   32   __   19   __   10   **5**

Now go to the Progress Chart to record your score!   Total   **85**

Mixed paper 2

Find the two letters that will end the first word and start the second word.

Example   pas (<u>ta</u>) ste

1 befo (__ __) ason   4 lem (__ __) ly

2 clo (__ __) ere   5 prin (__ __) iling

3 oli (__ __) st   **5**

If the code for HEALTHY is ? & * % ^ ? ! what do the following codes stand for?

6 ? & * ^   _____

8 % * ^ & % !   _____

7 ^ * % %   _____

Using the same code, what are the codes for the following words?

9 ALLY   _____

10 TEETH   _____

5

Underline the one word in the brackets which will go equally well with each of the words outside the brackets.

Example   word, paragraph, sentence   (pen, cap, <u>letter</u>, top, stop)

11 sun, rain, cloud   (water, weather, shine, dawn, grey)

12 Toyota, Ford, Vauxhall   (car, bike, train, country, garage)

13 lamb, pork, beef   (sheep, field, shop, chicks, meat)

14 heel, toe, ankle   (finger, knuckle, joint, foot, elbow)

15 lily, cannon, ice   (cube, flower, water, ball, gun)

5

Find the missing letters. The alphabet has been written out to help you.

A B C D E F G H I J K L M N O P Q R S T U V W X Y Z

Example   AB is to CD as PQ is to <u>RS</u>.

16 GH is to KL as OP is to _____.   **19** AQ is to BR as CS is to _____.

17 NL is to JH as FD is to _____.   **20** EC is to DB as CA is to _____.

18 EV is to GT as DW is to _____.

5

Match these words to the codes below:

FEET   FATE   FINE   NEAT   NINE

21 ⑥⑨⑥⑩   _____

24 ⑤⑩⑩④   _____

22 ⑤⑨⑥⑩   _____

25 ⑤❸④⑩   _____

23 ⑥⑩❸④   _____

5

Fill in the crosswords so that all the given words are included. You have been given one or two letters as a clue in each crossword.

25

26

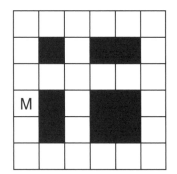

27

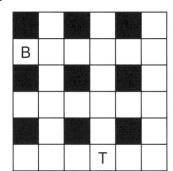

ROLLER RATHER RAREST
FATHER FARMER THRILL

CRATER BUTTER ATTEND
MUTTER STREET TRADER

If the code for FLUTTER is a v y h h o p, what do the following codes stand for?

28 h p y o _____   **30** v o h h o p _____

29 a v y a a _____

Remove one letter from the word in capital letters to leave a new word. The meaning of the new word is given in the clue.

Example AUNT   an insect   <u>ant</u>

31 BLAST   final   _____

32 SPRING   stem   _____

33 GRAIN   obtain   _____

34 BLEAKER   cup   _____

35 PAINTS   aches   _____

Underline the two words, one from each group, which are the most opposite in meaning.

Example (dawn, <u>early</u>, wake)   (<u>late,</u> stop, sunrise)

36 (dim, clever, torn)   (tattered, bright, folded)

37 (mild, cruel, beat)   (harsh, weak, thrash)

38 (better, wicked, rough)   (ready, good, smother)

39 (naught, icy, heat)   (zero, cool, warm)

40 (ours, mine, hole)   (dig, complete, theirs)

Find the two missing numbers in the following sequences.

Example 2 4 6 8 <u>10</u> <u>12</u>

41 3 6 12 __ __ 96

44 18 3 18 5 __ __

42 1 3 __ 7 9 __

45 6 4 __ 3 8 __

43 66 __ 44 33 __ 11

Rearrange the muddled words in capital letters so that each sentence makes sense.

Example There are sixty SNODCES <u>seconds</u> in a UTMINE <u>minute</u>.

46 Why can't you SECLO _____ the door YLTUQIE _____ ?

47 My REMTOH _____ went to the KTEMASPREUR _____ after dropping us at school.

48 In the DSYAHLOI _____, Petra NDEJIO _____ a swimming club.

49 The RATIN _____ stopped at many NSATTIOS _____ before we reached London.

50 After KRAEB _____, we have double YRHSOTI _____.

Underline two words, one from each group, that go together to form a new word. The word in the first group always comes first.

Example (hand, <u>green</u>, for)   (light, <u>house</u>, sure)

51 (plate, cup, chair)   (hair, form, board)

52 (good, bad, by)   (bye, by, buy)

53 (sail, law, fry)   (or, day, year)

54 (were, there, three)   (four, for, fore)

55 (for, in, out)   (cyst, cars, cast)

Underline the one word in each group which **can be made** from the letters of the word in capital letters.

Example CHAMPION   camping   notch   peach   cramp   <u>chimp</u>

56 CARDINAL   larder   danger   cranial   cradle   crayon

57 PREJUDICE   priced   justice   prelude   juicier   erudite

58	PARTICULAR	article	carpal	claret	particle	plural
59	GREATNESS	secret	nastier	agrees	stains	treats
60	YESTERDAY	sturdy	Saturday	strays	starry	trades

⬤ 5

Look at the first group of three words. The word in the middle has been made from the two other words. Complete the second group of three words in the same way, making a new word in the middle.

Example PAIN	INTO	TOOK	ALSO	<u>SOON</u>	ONLY
61 KERB	BRAN	NAPE	SOUP	_____	AMID
62 TALK	LATE	LOBE	LEFT	_____	NAIL
63 BONE	BEST	DUST	CURL	_____	BLUE
64 MIST	FIST	FISH	BEAM	_____	CALF
65 LIVE	LOVE	VOLE	ZOOM	_____	LIME

⬤ 5

Read the first two statements and then underline one of the four options below that must be true.

66 'Not all trees have green leaves. The ash tree has green leaves.'

   A Leaves fall from the trees in winter.

   B Many trees have green leaves.

   C Beech trees may have copper leaves.

   D Ash trees may have many leaves.

67 'Animals are either tame or wild. If animals are scared, they may bite.'

   A Wild animals always bite.

   B Tame animals never bite.

   C Wild animals may bite.

   D Wild animals are scared.

⬤ 2

68 If the seasons are put in alphabetical order, which season comes after summer? _____

69 Write the letters of the word COMPARE in alphabetical order.

_____

70 Using the answer for question 69 above, which is now the middle letter? _____

3

Change the first word into the last word, by changing one letter at a time and making a new, different word in the middle.

Example   CASE   <u>CASH</u>   LASH

71 KING   _____   FIND

72 SPOT   _____   HOOT

73 PURR   _____   CURE

74 SIFT   _____   LIFE

75 CORK   _____   COLD   5

If T = 3, L = 6, R = 5, B = 2, E = 1 and A = 4, find the sum of these words when the letters are added together.

76 TABLE _____   **77** LABEL _____   **78** RABBLE _____

79 Using the same code, if the total of BLADDER is 34, work out the value of D. _____

80 Using the same code, if the total of TRAILER is 31, work out the value of I. _____   5

Underline the two words in each line which are made from the same letters.

Example   TAP   PET   <u>TEA</u>   POT   <u>EAT</u>

81 ASLEEP   PLATER   TAILOR   LAPSES   PLEASE

82 TESTER   TASTER   STREET   STEERS   ASTERS

83 SNAILS   SPINAL   PLAINS   PALEST   STABLE

84 BITERS   STRIPE   PRISES   SPORES   TRIBES

85 BLEEPS   CHAPEL   PEBBLE   PLEACH   BLEACH   5

Now go to the Progress Chart to record your score!   Total   85

Mixed paper 3

Underline the one word in the brackets which will go with the word outside the brackets in the same way as the first two words go together.

Example good, better   bad, (naughty, worst, <u>worse</u>, nasty)

1 apple, pip   plum, (seed, stone, weed, tree)

2 quick, slow   flat, (house, fast, bumpy, room)

3 dog, kennel   cow, (barn, grass, milk, house)

4 bite, tooth   hold, (have, tongue, hand, nail)

5 six, three   four, (legs, five, eight, two)   **5**

If $p = 6$, $q = 3$, $r = 2$, $s = 5$, $t = 4$ and $u = 12$, work out the values of these calculations. Write each answer as a letter.

6 $pq - qr$ = _____   9 $p^2 \div q$ = _____

7 $(s + t) - p$ = _____   10 $tp - st$ = _____

8 $(u \div t) + (s - r)$ = _____   **5**

Match these codes to the words below.

a y i u   u i a a   a o u i   u o a y

11 STEM   _____   13 SAME   _____

12 MAST   _____   14 MESS   _____

15 Using the same code, what does y i o u stand for? _____   **5**

Find the four-letter word which can be added to the letters in capitals to make a new word. The new word will complete the sentence sensibly.

Example They enjoyed the BCAST. <u>ROAD</u>

16 Mrs Blunt took her shopping ET and went off to the shops.

_____

17 The little mouse SERED quickly back to its hole. _____

18 That coat is not yours; it BES to Yumi. _____

19 Mr Brown is angry as he is having trouble TING his car.

_____

20 On her birthday, Dad gave Mum a huge bunch of ERS. _____   **5**

Find the letter which will complete both pairs of words, ending the first word and starting the second. The same letter must be used for both pairs of words.

Focus test 1

1 rush, hurry
2 number, numeral
3 dog, wolf
4 by, near
5 hard, tough
6 brother, sister
7 raise
8 hate
9 rude
10 quick
11 minute
12 truth
13 bed
14 grey
15 Leeds
16 beech
17 contents
18 light
19 brave   timid
20 up   down
21 dry   wet
22 similar   opposite
23 happy   sad
24 find   lose
25 alert
26 sloping
27 perform
28 be
29 sprint
30 pace

Focus test 2

1 rule
2 watch
3 clip
4 light
5 sweet
6 current
7 CAR
8 ATE
9 THE
10 DEN
11 YOU
12 USE
13 zebra   safely
14 cricket   poured
15 street   bargains
16 branches   moving
17 stopped   station
18 everyone   laugh
19 instance
20 father
21 upstart
22 highlight
23 another
24 often
25 up
26 pop

27 blood
28 out
29 hood
30 blow

Focus test 3

1 g
2 b
3 f
4 a
5 c
6 w
7 n
8 r
9 e
10 se
11 in
12 ic
13 ch
14 t
15 y
16 b
17 k
18 plan   least
19 rift   heard
20 reason   steam
21 patter   pearl
22 fright   feed
23 heard
24 bitter
25 stuck
26 boast
27 potter
28 anger
29 pickle
30 wry

Focus test 4

1 crayon   ornament
2 clock   watch
3 giraffe   bear
4 stay   remain
5 educate   exercise
6 engine   elephant
7 rain
8 lead
9 limes
10 look
11 item
12 pane
13 church
14 engine
15 treats
16 dawning
17 grandly
18 broom
19 DUSTY   STUDY
20 STABLE   BLEATS
21 TOWELS   LOWEST
22 PRIEST   STRIPE

23 STORES   SOREST
24 LEARNT   ANTLER
25 hero
26 ache
27 fort
28 dash
29 them
30 soft

Focus test 5

1 REST
2 STOP
3 MIME
4 BOTH
5 RAID
6 CROW
7 SITS
8 FROM
9 CARD
10 PEAK
11 MICE
12 TEAR
13 PINT
14 BEAN
15 HURL
16 GRAB
17 PRAM
18 BAKE
19 CAKE
20 FIRE
21 SICK   SUCK
22 LOAD   LORD
23 WIRE   FIRE
24 LOFT   LOUT
25 LOOK   LOCK
26 TOLL   TOLD
27 TRIP   TRAP
28 FOOL   FOUL
29 LINE   FINE
30 FALL   FAIL

Focus test 6

1 2
2 14
3 4
4 2
5 8
6 E
7 A
8 14
9 12
10 11
11 C
12 D
13 Tina
14 Jo
15 Anya
16 2
17 3
18 1

19 5
20 4
21 SOLIHULL
22 SWANSEA
23 STOCKPORT
24 FRIDAY
25 WEDNESDAY
26 MONDAY
27 SUNDAY
28 A
29 G
30 N

Focus test 7

1 5 7 3 9
2 2 1 8 6
3 TEAR
4 TRUE
5 L Z O K K
6 SPEED
7 ↙ ← ↓ →
8 ROOT
9 NOUN
10 @ P 8 X
11 BEAR
12 BARB
13 REED
14 BARE
15 READ
16 E J C K T
17 BOOKS
18 R P C C Q
19 GRILL
20 8978
21 ABIDE
22 T G J Q U
23 X N K B G
24 VOGUE
25 TIMES
26 A D C Q B
27 HAPPY
28 S G Z T R
29 VALUE
30 A C X Z

Focus test 8

1 cold   hot
2 bark   person
3 heart   spade
4 clever   thick
5 TU
6 NM
7 AY
8 DS
9 TT
10 Ea
11 DW
12 AT
13 MN   PQ
14 ZY   RQ

15	ZA	HI
16	BZ	XV
17	NG	NK
18	EW	YV
19	MC	PA
20	ZF	TI
21	PKx	CLy
22	27	31
23	13	7
24	35	10
25	4	16
26	8	3
27	10	15
28	12	35
29	6	8
30	8	11

Mixed paper 1

1 glide, soar
2 prick, pierce
3 crowd, throng
4 select, choose
5 poor, unfortunate
6 SHE
7 TEA
8 HOE
9 FOR
10 HIS
11 s
12 f
13 w
14 e
15 r
16 hill, mountain
17 tap, map
18 left, wrong
19 on, inside
20 Mediterranean, North
21 DOGS
22 SING
23 KEEP
24 SNIP
25 MUGS
26 5
27 18
28 3
29 5
30 4
31 3 5 2 7
32 7 5 2 4
33 4 1 7 7 5 3
34 HOPING
35 HIGH
36 glass, door
37 high, low
38 horse, sheep
39 kitchen, bath
40 toe, arm
41 fright
42 sport
43 beard

44 pleat
45 carve
46 surfboard
47 waterproof
48 backward
49 begun
50 capable
51 HARM
52 SNUG
53 LIFE
54 SLOW
55 MATE
56 tennis balls
57 footballs
58 cricket balls
59 hockey balls
60 rugby balls
61 faint
62 cruel
63 mad
64 brave
65 hate
66 e
67 z
68 k
69 l
70 f
71 nasty
72 grand
73 ladles
74 chant
75 trump
76 DRAG
77 RANG
78 NEAR
79 GREEN
80 GRADE

81	27	47
82	2	4
83	30	18
84	9	18
85	25	14

Mixed paper 2

1 re
2 th
3 ve
4 on
5 ce
6 HEAT
7 TALL
8 LATELY
9 * % % !
10 ^ & & ^ ?
11 weather
12 car
13 meat
14 foot
15 water
16 ST
17 BZ

18 FU
19 DT
20 BZ
21 NINE
22 FINE
23 NEAT
24 FEET
25 FATE
26

```
F A T H E R
A ▪ H ▪ ▪ A
R A R E S T
M ▪ I ▪ ▪ H
E ▪ L ▪ ▪ E
R O L L E R
```

27

```
▪ M S ▪ ▪ T
B U T T E R
▪ T ▪ R ▪ A
A T T E N D
E ▪ ▪ E ▪ E
C R A T E R
```

28 TRUE
29 FLUFF
30 LETTER
31 last
32 sprig
33 gain
34 beaker
35 pains
36 dim   bright
37 mild   harsh
38 wicked   good
39 heat   cool
40 ours   theirs
41 24   48
42 5   11
43 55   22
44 18   7
45 7   2
46 close   quietly
47 mother   supermarket
48 holidays   joined
49 train   stations
50 break   history
51 cupboard
52 goodbye
53 sailor
54 therefore
55 outcast
56 cranial
57 priced
58 carpal
59 agrees
60 trades
61 PUMA
62 FELL
63 CLUE
64 CALM

65 MILE
66 B
67 C
68 WINTER
69 ACEMOPR
70 M
71 KIND
72 SOOT
73 PURE
74 LIFT
75 CORD
76 16
77 19
78 20
79 8
80 7
81 ASLEEP   PLEASE
82 TESTER   STREET
83 SPINAL   PLAINS
84 BITERS   TRIBES
85 CHAPEL   PLEACH

Mixed paper 3

1 stone
2 bumpy
3 barn
4 hand
5 two
6 u
7 q
8 p
9 u
10 t
11 a y i u
12 u o a y
13 a o u i
14 u i a a
15 TEAM
16 BASK
17 CAMP
18 LONG
19 STAR
20 FLOW
21 e
22 p
23 z
24 t
25 g
26 p
27 g
28 l
29 a
30 b
31 eight   equals
32 traffic   forwards
33 killed   chickens
34 rained   muddy
35 haircut   older
36 r 4 c 8
37 b r = 4 c =
38 b 4 r = c 8

39 LAPSE
40 APPLES
41 LM PQ
42 Yz Uz
43 IJ JK
44 ZB BD
45 CX GT
46 10 16
47 16 16
48 5 25
49 11 16
50 6 48
51 playground rain wet
52 Yesterday visit hospital
53 types fish sea
54 car car park shops
55 door open inside
56 seem
57 best
58 hall
59 tour
60 very
61 lay purge
62 quit every
63 ample hairs
64 beak drove
65 water fiend
66 fraction part
67 uncle son
68 March autumn
69 orange cereal
70 five one
71 C
72 E
73 A
74 D
75 B
76 DOTE DOVE
77 DAMP DAME
78 ROSY ROSE
79 LANE LAND
80 MILE MALE
81 cereals
82 tools
83 colours
84 computer
85 can

Mixed paper 4

1 bran
2 stained
3 bought
4 hated
5 stand
6 tribe
7 flower
8 dances
9 chives
10 solvent
11 18
12 24
13 23
14 A
15 C
16 ignite, light
17 dwell, live
18 easy, simple
19 lift, elevate
20 under, below
21 strong
22 evil
23 cooled
24 lean
25 sane
26 godfather
27 background
28 into
29 overboard
30 behold
31 FOUR
32 NINE
33 ZERO
34 FIVE
35 F H H G U
36 blew
37 them
38 feel
39 chap
40 this
41 fire
42 ward
43 out
44 gold
45 man
46 BLOW
47 TINT
48 GOLD
49 HOLE
50 HARD
51 brick glass
52 calm call
53 four man
54 road rails
55 chapter verse
56 62 102
57 2 15
58 5 7
59 15 8
60 25 17
61 JOKE
62 EARN
63 GRIT
64 HALO
65 KING
66 en
67 er
68 ee
69 st
70 es
71 hot roads melting
72 through quietly hear
73 slipped icy arm
74 track uneven puddles
75 colour red post boxes
76 V J T Q Y
77 N Y Q R Y
78 YEARN
79 APRIL
80 MARCH
81 BOLIVIA
82 BULGARIA
83 BOTSWANA
84

B	A	N	T	E	R
	T		R		E
R	O	W	I	N	G
	N		L		E
M	E	R	L	I	N
	S		S		T

85

P	A	R	A	D	E
A		E		R	
S	A	L	T	E	D
T		I		D	
R	A	V	A	G	E
Y		E		E	

Mixed paper 5

1 leave in place
2 watched programme cities
3 shining brightly window
4 book reading exciting
5 shop rotten buy
6 same
7 dry
8 inner
9 low
10 vanish
11 autumn leaves
12 bonfire night
13 football sport
14 pencil working
15 capital England
16 4 9 3 5
17 6 1 3 5 4
18 2 1 4 7 5
19 HEDGE
20 CABBAGE
21 n
22 h
23 l
24 d
25 s
26 ROSE
27 SIRE
28 SHIP
29 HEAR
30 THIN
31 ignite
32 dragon
33 drained
34 crusts
35 shelter
36 22
37 A
38 B
39 24
40 D
41 brush spade
42 see ear
43 punishment reward
44 pursue trust
45 paw talon
46 D
47 G
48 R
49 N
50 H
51 LICE
52 BEAR
53 FULL
54 RAIN
55 RAGE
56 C B P M W
57 NIGHT
58 AWAKE
59 M J F I S
60 Q N T S X
61 finish start
62 deep shallow
63 clean dirty
64 blunt sharp
65 pull push
66 fore
67 wire
68 hub
69 suck
70 dare
71 CHIP
72 BRED
73 MEAN 74 HUSH
75 CHAT 76 rear
77 mesh 78 then
79 tone 80 sour
81 A8 B9
82 DJ PB
83 IR HT
84 DE FG
85 YE AC

Mixed paper 6

1 LEAF
2 WASP
3 DIRT
4 EACH
5 PLEA

6

D	E	B	A	T	E
O		O		A	
U	N	R	O	L	L
B		R		K	
L	O	O	K	E	D
E		W		D	

7

T	A	L	E	N	T
A		E		I	
V	O	T	I	N	G
E		H		E	
R	E	A	C	T	S
N		L		Y	

8 C
9 P
10 R
11 PX RZ
12 MM NP
13 PP VY
14 ZA YB
15 BQ AW
16 SNOWY
17 H Z U D T
18 ROADS
19 Z E B T P
20 R T R H N
21 4 4
22 1 2
23 12 21
24 11 8
25 11 9
26 V
27 W
28 Y
29 Z
30 W
31 A
32 2
33 D
34 C
35 one
36 pod
37 grave
38 won
39 bake
40 than
41 charm, allure
42 fix, attach
43 insane, senseless
44 move, shift
45 stick, adhere
46 side
47 high
48 man
49 horse
50 slip
51 over
52 pet

53 quick
54 grey
55 ram
56 bacon snipe
57 with chair
58 stale bringing
59 chin bread
60 nigh meant
61 height
62 tall
63 lesser
64 trap
65 pane
66 LAMENT MENTAL
67 REPORT PORTER
68 DRIEST STRIDE
69 LATENT TALENT
70 LEADER DEALER
71 HARD
72 TALE
73 DISH
74 COME
75 DEAD
76 B B U F R
77 STEEP
78 F S Z J M
79 STALL
80 E V Y A X
81 they
82 down 83 reel
84 oral 85 chop

Mixed paper 7

1 stale 2 cat
3 trait 4 to
5 chum 6 way
7 light 8 pine
9 slack 10 wind
11 great 12 green
13 ball
14

T	I	P	T	O	E
	C		O		N
P	I	C	K	L	E
	C		E		R
	L		N		G
F	E	I	S	T	Y

15

P	R	A	Y	E	R
	A		O		E
	T		U		A
S	T	A	T	U	S
	L		H		O
S	E	A	S	O	N

16 HAND
17 HARD
18 DASH
19 SAND

20 S Z T G
21 TALE TALL
22 RIFT RAFT
23 SHOW SLOW
24 SPUR SPUN
25 RAVE HAVE
26 bare, naked
27 climb, ascend
28 steal, rob
29 pig, hog
30 pardon, forgive
31 FF JH
32 ZE BI
33 TB KA
34 ZX XA
35 ZA AZ
36 care
37 for
38 house
39 cart
40 leg
41 E R A H V
42 O N T D T
43 GIRLS
44 VILLA 45 STRAW
46 STORK 47 SWIFT
48 A 49 G
50 N 51 RICK
52 ABLE 53 ICED
54 RAKE 55 EDGE
56 bust 57 also
58 tour 59 them
60 ours 61 support
62 foot 63 times
64 toenail 65 case
66 F 67 L
68 O 69 E
70 O 71 th
72 ex 73 se
74 ea 75 al
76 XW 77 ID
78 EH 79 MN
80 JQ 81 NODE
82 SALE 83 SITE
84 FROG 85 SUCH

Mixed paper 8

1 X Z U D S
2 HOSES
3 BLACK
4 Q J Y F C
5 G M P P E
6 wing
7 black
8 hide
9 bolt
10 key
11 FAME FUME
12 TWIN THIN
13 WASH WISH
14 FACE FADE

15 MOON NOON
16 DE
17 DW
18 DH
19 VB
20 WB
21 R T F D O
22 H T W K V
23 JEANS
24 Q X M S B
25 LARGE
26 ate
27 lime
28 keep
29 slit
30 overt
31 sparkling
32 play
33 uneven 34 bruise
35 cut 36 OMEN
37 WEEP 38 VEST
39 TOMB 40 NAIL
41 TART 42 LASH
43 RIPE 44 AGED
45 HOSE 46 ours
47 land 48 herb
49 rest 50 then
51 XX TT
52 MO LL
53 MP YB
54 TY IJ
55 RB GV
56 chair, sofa
57 purple, violet
58 leopard, lion
59 kind, sort
60 gesture, signal
61 N
62 H
63 T
64 BLACK
65 GREY
66 red
67 green
68 Micah
69 Sarah
70 Sam
71 ar
72 op
73 ch
74 ce
75 un
76 skin
77 apostrophe
78 centimetre
79 bread
80 metal
81 hound
82 show
83 side
84 pay
85 man

Example mea (<u>t</u>) able   fi (<u>t</u>) ub

21 bit (_) ach   hat (_) very   24 sea (_) op   mea (_) win

22 fla (_) ony   tra (_) et   25 dra (_) host   sin (_) et

23 qui (_) ip   buz (_) oo   5

Which one letter can be added to the front of all of these words to make new words?

Example <u>c</u>are   <u>c</u>at   <u>c</u>rate   <u>c</u>all

26 __art   __each   __arched   __ink

27 __asp   __rate   __lad   __row

28 __and   __ink   __ate   __imp

29 __we   __sleep   __cross   __head

30 __lock   __low   __ear   __army   5

Rearrange the muddled words in capital letters so that each sentence makes sense.

Example There are sixty SNODCES <u>seconds</u> in a UTMINE <u>minute</u>.

31 HTEIG _____ plus seven QLSUEA _____ fifteen.

32 The green CTRIAFF _____ light allows cars to move
    WFRODSAR _____.

33 Last night, a fox LDELKI _____ our HCCKNEIS _____.

34 As it has DRAINE _____ hard, the park will be very YDUMD
    _____.

35 Maisy's new RCHTUIA _____ makes her look much DLORE
    _____.   5

If the code for STAPLE is c 8 4 b r =, what are the codes for the following words?

36 LAST   _____   38 PALEST   _____

37 PLEASE   _____

Using the same code, what do the following codes stand for?

39 r 4 b c = _____   40 4 b b r = c _____   5

Find the two missing pairs of letters in the following sequences.

A B C D E F G H I J K L M N O P Q R S T U V W X Y Z

Example CQ   DP   EQ   FP   <u>GQ</u>   <u>HP</u>

41 JK   __   NO   __   RS   TU

42 Zz   __   Xz   Wz   Vz   __

43 GH   HI   __   __   KL   LM

44 __   AC   __   CE   DF   EG

45 __   DW   EV   FU   __   HS   ⬤ 5

Find the two missing numbers in the following sequences.

Example 2   4   6   8   <u>10</u>   <u>12</u>

46 7   __   13   __   19   22

47 15   __   __   14   17   12

48 __   10   15   20   __   30

49 1   2   4   7   __   __

50 3   __   12   24   __   96   ⬤ 5

Complete the following sentences by selecting the most sensible word from each group of words given in the brackets. Underline the words selected.

Example The (<u>children</u>, boxes, foxes) carried the (houses, <u>books</u>, steps) home from the (greengrocer, <u>library</u>, factory).

51 We cannot go out into the (playground, classroom, bedroom) as it is pouring with (fire, rain, snow) and we will get very (tired, hot, wet).

52 (Yesterday, Tomorrow, Today) afternoon we went to (annoy, climb, visit) a friend who is sick in (hospital, cinema, fire station).

53 There are many (types, cans, envelopes) of (cows, fish, paper) that live in the (house, sea, jar).

54 Mum parked the (horse, car, train) in the (pond, car park, hedge) next to the (shops, swan, kettle).

55 As the (book, door, mouth) was (wide, open, speaking) she went (inside, outside, over) without knocking.   ⬤ 5

Find the four-letter word hidden at the end of one word and the beginning of the next word. The order of the letters may not be changed.

Example We had ba<u>ts and</u> balls. <u>sand</u>

56 Please empty your rubbish bin over here. _____

57 The cat is asleep and doesn't want to be stroked. _____

58 At break time we played with all the little children. _____

59 We met our new next door neighbours at the party. _____

60 I could see your swing over your garden fence. _____   ⬤ 5

Move one letter from the first word and add it to the second word to make two new words.

Example hunt   sip   <u>hut</u>   <u>snip</u>

61 play   urge   _____   _____

62 quite   very   _____   _____

63 sample   hair   _____   _____

64 break   dove   _____   _____

65 waiter   fend   _____   _____   ⬤ 5

Underline the two words which are the odd ones out in the following groups of words.

Example black   <u>king</u>   purple   green   <u>house</u>

66 whole	fraction	entire	complete	part
67 uncle	wife	daughter	grandmother	son
68 Monday	March	Saturday	autumn	Friday
69 orange	cauliflower	carrot	cereal	courgette
70 sixteen	five	one	eight	four

⬤ 5

On a garden rockery, there were seven stones. Under each stone lived a different type of small animal. From the clues and the diagram, work out where each type of animal lived.

LEFT				RIGHT	
A				SNAILS	TOP
	B		C		
CENTIPEDES		D		E	BOTTOM

The snails were not directly above the woodlice.

The beetles were on a row somewhere above the woodlice.

The centipedes were on the same row as the worms.

The earwigs were on the same row as the slugs, which are closer to the centipedes than the earwigs.

71 earwigs   _____   74 woodlice   _____

72 worms   _____   75 slugs   _____   ⬤ 5

73 beetles   _____

Change the first word into the last word, by changing one letter at a time and making two new, different words in the middle.

Example   CASE   <u>CASH</u>   <u>WASH</u>   WISH

76 VOTE   _____   _____   DIVE

77 RAMP   _____   _____   DIME

78 COSY   _____   _____   ROVE

79 LATE   _____   _____   LEND

80 MILK   _____   _____   KALE   ⬤ 5

Underline the one word in the brackets which will go equally well with each of the words outside the brackets.

Example   word, paragraph, sentence   (pen, cap, <u>letter</u>, top, stop)

81 wheat, oats, bran   (breakfast, cereals, grass, bread, milk)

82 spanner, hammer, saw   (tools, nail, screw, wood, mend)

83 indigo, brown, red   (paint, rainbow, sky, lights, colours)

84 keys, mouse, screen   (lock, trap, wide, computer, mobile)

85 mug, waste paper basket, barrel   (roll, tea, watering can, ball, cannot)   ⬤ 5

Remove one letter from the word in capital letters to leave a new word. The meaning of the new word is given in the clue.

Example AUNT   an insect   <u>ant</u>

1 BRAND   fibre   _____

2 STRAINED   marked   _____

3 BROUGHT   purchased   _____

4 HEATED   loathed   _____

5 STRAND   upright   _____   **5**

Underline the one word in each group which **can be made** from the letters of the word in capital letters.

Example CHAMPION camping notch   peach   cramp   <u>chimp</u>

6 BRIGHTEN   gender   rights   tribe   better   nightie

7 POWERFUL   flower   proof   parole   leper   prefer

8 DISTANCE   canter   stains   dances   stands   insist

9 VEHICLES   sieves   sleek   leaves   wheels   chives

10 TELEVISION   notelet   hotels   notice   solvent   noises   **5**

If $t = 4$, $c = 7$, $r = 3$, $a = 1$, $l = 5$, $e = 6$ and $w = 2$, find the sum of these words when the letters are added together.

11 crawl   _____

13 wallet   _____

12 crater   _____   **3**

Read the first two statements and then underline one of the four options below that must be true.

14 'Madrid is the capital of Spain. Spain is in Europe.'

A Madrid is a European city.

B England is in Europe.

C The euro is the currency for much of Europe.

D People from Spain speak Spanish.

15 'A robin is a type of bird. Birds have feathers.'

    A Robins are good at flying.   **C** Robins have feathers.

    B Robins have red breasts.   **D** All birds are robins.

2

Underline the pair of words which are the most similar in meaning.

Example come, go   <u>roams, wanders</u>   fear, fare

  16 ignite, light   pale, dark   night, day

  17 life, death   dwell, live   fetch, carry

  18 true, false   easy, simple   tough, clear

  19 lift, elevate   drop, leave   come, go

  20 up, down   over, through   under, below

5

Find the word that is opposite in meaning to the word in capital letters and that rhymes with the second word.

Example SHARP   front   <u>blunt</u>

  21 FRAIL   long   _____

  22 GOOD   weevil   _____

  23 HEATED   ruled   _____

  24 PLUMP   seen   _____

  25 CRAZY   drain   _____

5

Underline two words, one from each group, that go together to form a new word. The word in the first group always comes first.

Example (hand, <u>green</u>, for)   (light, <u>house</u>, sure)

  26 (good, god, grade)   (further, father, future)

  27 (back, four, head)   (plain, ground, grass)

  28 (in, and, who)   (to, be, how)

  29 (over, oven, order)   (line, law, board)

  30 (in, out, be)   (hold, hive, port)

5

If the code for STORM is T S P Q N, match the right code to each word given below.

ZERO   FOUR   FIVE   NINE

31 G N V Q _____ **33** A D S N _____

32 O H O D _____ **34** G H W D _____

35 What would EIGHT be, using the same code? _____ **5**

Find the four-letter word hidden at the end of one word and the beginning of the next word. The order of the letters may not be changed.

Example We had bats_ and_ balls. _sand_

36 Calm down and try explaining in a quiet and sensible way.

_____

37 As the weather worsened, the mountains disappeared from view.

_____

38 Tea and coffee leave me feeling thirsty. _____

39 We looked carefully for blemishes on each apple. _____

40 Conrad left his jacket on the floor of the gym. _____ **5**

Find a word that can be put either in front or at the end of each of the following words to make new, compound words.

Example cast   fall   ward   pour   _down_

41 cracker   ball   fighter   side   _____

42 for   back   in   up   _____

43 doors   back   look   grow   _____

44 finch   fish   smith   field   _____

45 age   kind   hood   or   _____ **5**

Change the first word into the last word, by changing one letter at a time and making a new, different word in the middle.

Example CASE   _CASH_   LASH

46 BROW   _____   SLOW

47 TINY   _____   TILT

48 GOOD   _____   BOLD

49 HOME   _____   HOLT

50 YARD   _____   HARK **5**

Complete the following sentences in the best way by choosing one word from each set of brackets.

Example Tall is to (tree, short, colour) as narrow is to (thin, white, wide).

51 House is to (roof, door, brick) as greenhouse is to (glass, small, plants).

52 Belt is to bell as (calm, ramp, find) is to (damp, call, farm).

53 Cat is to (fur, four, mouse) as (man, hat, number) is to two.

54 Lorry is to (big, car, road) as train is to (rails, passenger, ticket).

55 Book is to (chapter, novel, title) as poem is to (verse, word, rhyme).

⬤ 5

Find the two missing numbers in the following sequences.

Example 2 4 6 8 <u>10</u> <u>12</u>

56 2 22 42 __ 82 __

57 __ __ 6 13 10 11

58 __ 3 4 5 3 __

59 26 20 __ 11 __ 6

60 29 __ 21 __ 13 9

⬤ 5

Look at the first group of three words. The word in the middle has been made from the two other words. Complete the second group of three words in the same way, making a new word in the middle.

Example PAIN <u>IN</u>TO <u>TO</u>OK ALSO <u>SOON</u> ONLY

61 JERK PORK PONY MAKE _____ JOIN

62 CLAW LAWN NOTE WEAR _____ NAIL

63 HOOF FISH SIFT TANG _____ IRON

64 CALL ALSO SOLD WHAT _____ LOOK

65 LIMB BONE ZONE HUSK _____ WING

⬤ 5

Find the two letters that will end the first word and start the second word.

Example pas (<u>ta</u>) ste

66 brok (__ __) joy

67 tend (__ __) ect

68 agr (__ __) rie

69 fir (__ __) amp

70 bus (__ __) say

⬤ 5

Complete the following sentences by selecting the most sensible word from each group of words given in the brackets. Underline the words selected.

Example The (<u>children</u>, boxes, foxes) carried the (houses, <u>books</u>, steps) home from the (greengrocer, <u>library</u>, factory).

71 It is so (hot, cold, rainy) today that the tarmac on the (roads, bikes, deer) is (swimming, crying, melting).

72 The lioness crept (up, with, through) the long grass so (quietly, loudly, kindly) the deer did not see or (touch, hear, laugh) her coming.

73 Poor Alvina (slipped, laughed, sang) on the (icy, green, pretty) step and fell and broke her (father, water, arm).

74 The (track, elevator, ladder) to the farm was rough and (level, uneven, easy) with large, muddy (puddles, spiders, boots).

75 My favourite (bed, colour, cat) is (high, spotty, red) like the colour of (post boxes, caravans, pillows).

5

76 If the code for CATCH is E C V E J, what is the code for THROW?
_____

77 If the code for LUNCH is J S L A F, what is the code for PASTA?
_____

78 If the code for WANTS is Z D Q W V, what does B H D U Q stand for?
_____

3

If the code for AUGUST is Z V F V R U, what do the following codes stand for?

79 Z Q Q J K _____   80 L B Q D G _____

2

BULGARIA   BELGIUM   BOTSWANA   BOLIVIA   BURUNDI

If these countries are put in alphabetical order, which comes:

81 second? _____   82 fourth? _____   83 after Bolivia? _____

3

Fill in the crosswords so that all the given words are included. You have been given one letter as a clue in each crossword.

39

84

REGENT   BANTER   TRILLS

ROWING   MERLIN   ATONES

85

PASTRY   PARADE   DREDGE

RAVAGE   SALTED   RELIVE

2

Now go to the Progress Chart to record your score!   Total   85

Mixed paper 5

Complete the following sentences by selecting the most sensible word from each group of words given in the brackets. Underline the words selected.

Example The (<u>children</u>, boxes, foxes) carried the (houses, <u>books</u>, steps) home from the (greengrocer, <u>library</u>, factory).

1 Please don't (leave, find, jump) me alone (in, through, over) this strange (place, colour, wolf).

2 Yesterday we (ate, watched, threw) an interesting (pizza, programme, spear) on animals living in our (cities, buckets, socks).

3 The moon is (shining, calling, falling) really (suddenly, brightly, quickly) through my bedroom (wall, road, window).

4 The (book, garage, bird) I am (reading, flying, mending) at the moment is very (exciting, swimming, driving).

5 The fruit in the (shop, bridge, cage) was either unripe or (rotten, unkind, pink) so my mother did not (eat, buy, wish) it.

5

Find the word that is opposite in meaning to the word in capital letters and that rhymes with the second word.

Example SHARP   front   <u>blunt</u>

6 DIFFERENT   blame   _____

7 WET   fly   _____

8 OUTER   dinner   _____

9 HIGH   sew   _____

10 APPEAR   banish   _____   ⬭ 5

Rearrange the muddled words in capital letters so that each sentence makes sense.

Example   There are sixty SNODCES <u>seconds</u> in a UTMINE <u>minute</u>.

11 In AUUMNT _____ many trees lose their VSELAE

_____.

12 The BFRENIO _____ burned brightly against the INHGT

_____ sky.

13 BFLTOALO _____ is my favourite PTORS _____ at
our school.

14 Her CLIPNE _____ kept breaking as she was GNIWRKO

_____.

15 London is the PTLACAI _____ city of GLAENDN

_____.   ⬭ 5

If the code for BEAD is 2 5 1 4, what are the codes for the following words?

16 DICE   _____   **18** BADGE   _____

17 FACED   _____

Using the same code, what do the following codes stand for?

19 8 5 4 7 5   _____   **20** 3 1 2 2 1 7 5   _____   ⬭ 5

Find the letter that will end the first word and start the second word.

Example   drow (<u>n</u>) ought

21 year (__) or   **24** hee (__) oor

22 bus (__) orror   **25** wa (__) wan

23 vea (__) ove   ⬭ 5

Change the first word into the last word, by changing one letter at a time and making a new, different word in the middle.

Example   CASE   <u>CASH</u>   LASH

26 HOSE	_____	ROBE	
27 SURE	_____	FIRE	
28 WHIP	_____	SLIP	
29 GEAR	_____	HEAP	
30 CHIN	_____	THAN	5

Underline the one word in each group which **cannot be made** from the letters of the word in capital letters.

Example STATIONERY   stone   tyres   ration   <u>nation</u>   noisy

31 LIGHTNING	glint	night	ignite	thing	tiling
32 GRANDEUR	danger	gander	ranger	dragon	grader
33 SPRAINED	drapes	rinsed	rained	drained	spared
34 CREATURES	steer	crusts	curate	traces	secret
35 BATTLESHIP	spittle	thistle	shape	tables	shelter

5

In a test at school out of 35, pupil A got 24 right while pupil B got 17 wrong. C got 10 less than D who got 4 more than B. E got half of A's score.

36 How many did D get right? _____

37 Who did the best? _____

38 Who got 6 more marks than C? _____

39 How many marks did C and E score when their totals are added together? _____

40 Who did better than B but not as well as A? _____

5

Complete the following sentences in the best way by choosing one word from each set of brackets.

Example Tall is to (tree, <u>short</u>, colour) as narrow is to (thin, white, <u>wide</u>).

41 Broom is to (brush, mop, hammer) as shovel is to (nail, fork, spade).

42 Eye is to (lash, see, face) as (ear, hair, foot) is to hear.

43 Crime is to (criminal, punishment, robber) as a good deed is to (reward, thief, problem).

44 Chase is to (pursue, catch, keep) as believe in is to (lie, trust, pray).

45 Wolf is to (howl, paw, hunt) as eagle is to (soar, talon, beak).

5

42

If the letters of the word TREADING are put into alphabetical order, which comes:

46 second? _____   **48** seventh? _____

47 fourth? _____

If the letters of the word CHAMPION are put into alphabetical order, which comes:

49 sixth? _____   **50** third? _____

5

Find the four-letter word which can be added to the letters in capitals to make a new word. The new word will complete the sentence sensibly.

Example   They enjoyed the BCAST. <u>ROAD</u>

51 Please may I have another S of cake? _____

52 Father Christmas is pictured with a bushy white D. _____

53 HOPEY it will stop raining soon. _____

54 Deserts are dry, arid places with little FALL. _____

55 My father has a workshop in the GA. _____

5

56 If the code for SLEEP is Q M C F N, what is the code for EARLY?

_____

57 Using the same code, what does L J E I R stand for? _____

58 If the code for DREAM is C S D B L, what does Z X Z L D stand for?

_____

59 Using the same code, what is the code for NIGHT? _____

60 If the code for TIGER is Y N L J W, what is the code for LIONS?

_____

5

Underline the two words, one from each group, which are the most opposite in meaning.

Example   (dawn, <u>early</u>, wake)   (<u>late</u>, stop, sunrise)

61 (surprise, finish, book)   (end, start, paper)

62 (deep, broad, high)   (steep, shallow, wide)

63 (grubby, clean, messy)   (dirty, chaos, dump)

64 (pencil, chalk, blunt)   (pen, sharp, feeble)

65 (pull, heave, choose)   (press, push, select)

5

Change the first word of the third pair in the same way as the other pairs to give a new word.

Example bind, hind   bare, hare   but, <u>hut</u>

66 comb, come   wand, wane   form, _____

67 type, tyre   pant, part   wine, _____

68 come, hum   with, hut   jibe, _____

69 lack, luck   tack, tuck   sack, _____

70 leap, pale   deaf, fade   read, _____   5

Look at the first group of three words. The word in the middle has been made from the two other words. Complete the second group of three words in the same way, making a new word in the middle.

Example PA<u>IN</u> INTO <u>TO</u>OK   ALSO   <u>SOON</u>   ONLY

71 BATH   THIN   WIND   RICH   _____   WIPE

72 FORT   TRIM   SLIM   KERB   _____   SPED

73 PEAR   READ   DAMP   GERM   _____   NAVY

74 ENDS   SHOE   HOME   HIGH   _____   USED

75 KITE   TERM   MORE   MUCH   _____   TRAP   5

Find the four-letter word hidden at the end of one word and the beginning of the next word. The order of the letters may not be changed.

Example We had bat<u>s and</u> balls. <u>sand</u>

76 Where are your clean clothes, Javin? _____

77 Tania will not be allowed to come shopping with you on Friday.

_____

78 A train clattered by noisily through the new level crossing.

_____

79 Paul put one of his paintings in an art exhibition. _____

80 A squirrel visits our bird table to gobble all the bird food. _____   5

Find the two missing pairs of letters in the following sequences.

A B C D E F G H I J K L M N O P Q R S T U V W X Y Z

Example CQ   DP   EQ   FP   <u>GQ</u>   <u>HP</u>

44

81	Y6	Z7	___	___	C10	D11
82	___	GH	JF	MD	___	SZ
83	HP	___	___	IV	HX	IZ
84	AB	BC	CD	___	EF	___
85	___	___	CA	EY	GW	IU

⊙ 5

Now go to the Progress Chart to record your score!　　Total　⊙ 85

Mixed paper 6

Look at the first group of three words. The word in the middle has been made from the two other words. Complete the second group of three words in the same way, making a new word in the middle.

Example	PA<u>IN</u>	INTO	<u>TO</u>OK	ALSO	<u>SOON</u>	ONLY
1	POSH	HOOP	SORT	FAIL	_____	FERN
2	BUSY	MUST	MINT	GASH	_____	WEEP
3	LOOK	KEEP	PEEK	LOAD	_____	TRIP
4	REEL	FEAR	LOAF	HOAX	_____	NICE
5	SNAP	DRIP	BIRD	PUMA	_____	HELP

⊙ 5

Fill in the crosswords so that all the given words are included. You have been given one letter as a clue in each crossword.

6

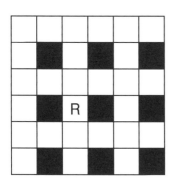

BORROW　LOOKED　UNROLL
TALKED　DOUBLE　DEBATE

7

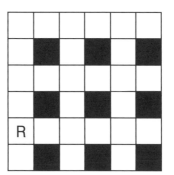

REACTS　TAVERN　TALENT
VOTING　NINETY　LETHAL

⊙ 2

45

If the letters of the word PICTURES are put into alphabetical order, which comes:

8 first? _____   **9** fourth? _____   **10** fifth? _____   ○ 3

Find the two missing pairs of letters in the following sequences.

A B C D E F G H I J K L M N O P Q R S T U V W X Y Z

Example CQ   DP   EQ   FP   <u>GQ</u>   <u>HP</u>

11 __   __   TB   VD   XF   ZH

12 MK   NL   __   NN   MO   __

13 NM   __   RS   TV   __   XB

14 CX   BY   AZ   __   __   XC

15 __   GM   LI   QE   VA   __   ○ 5

16 If the code for IGLOO is K F N N Q, what does U M Q V A stand for?

_____

17 If the code for FENCE is G D O B F, what is the code for GATES?

_____

18 If the code for CROSS is D S P T T, what does S P B E T stand for?

_____

19 If the code for BITES is Y F Q B P, what is the code for CHEWS?

_____

20 If the code for TEACH is V D C B J, what is the code for PUPIL?

_____   ○ 5

Find the two missing numbers in the following sequences.

Example 2 4 6 8 <u>10</u> <u>12</u>

21 8 2 6 3 __ __ 2 5   **24** 2 __ 4 8 6 5 __ 2

22 __ __ 4 7 11 16 22 29   **25** 10 13 __ 11 12 __ 13 7   ○ 5

23 3 6 9 __ 15 18 __ 24

If Z = 3, Y = 5, W = 10, V = 2 and U = 4, what are the values of these calculations? Write each answer as a letter.

26 (Z + Y) − (W − U) = _____   **28** $\dfrac{(Y + Z + W + V)}{U}$ = _____

27 (U² − Z²) + Z   = _____

29 $(VYZ) \div W =$ _____   **30** $ZW - YU =$ _____   5

At a football match, six friends all wore their red supporters' shirts. A and B wore hats but no scarves. C, F and E wore hats and scarves. B and D and E had flags and hats. A and C carried whistles.

31 Who had a whistle but no scarf? _____

32 How many friends wore hats and scarves but no whistles?

_____

33 Who, besides A and B, did not have a scarf? _____

34 Who had a hat, scarf and whistle? _____

35 How many wore scarves and carried flags? _____   5

Change the first word of the third pair in the same way as the other pairs to give a new word.

Example bind, hind   bare, hare   but, <u>hut</u>

36 gasp, gap   camp, cap   pond, _____

37 knit, knave   slow, slave   gruel, _____

38 pot, top   nit, tin   now, _____

39 food, fade   moon, mane   book, _____

40 crime, mean   stale, lean   broth, _____   5

Underline the pair of words which are the most similar in meaning.

Example come, go   <u>roams, wanders</u>   fear, fare

41 charm, allure   repel, avoid   dazzle, subdue

42 fix, attach   sew, needle   stitch, tapestry

43 mad, sane   insane, senseless   common, sense

44 remain, go   below, behind   move, shift

45 glue, tape   stick, adhere   paste, solid   5

Find a word that can be put either in front or at the end of each of the following words to make new, compound words.

Example cast   fall   ward   pour   <u>down</u>

46	out	in	be	a	_____
47	lighter	land	ball	way	_____
48	hole	age	servant	trap	_____
49	play	fly	power	back	_____
50	stream	per	ping	way	_____

5

Underline the one word in the brackets which will go equally well with both sets of words outside the brackets.

Example rush, attack   cost, fee   (price, hasten, strike, <u>charge</u>, money)

51 done, finished   cricketing term   (over, complete, wicket, century, ball)

52 domestic animal   stroke, pat   (cat, rabbit, fondle, pet, dog)

53 fast, swift   intelligent, sharp   (quick, rapid, clever, bright, cool)

54 a colour   dull, nondescript   (blue, yellow, black, grey, brown)

55 male sheep   pack, stuff   (ram, ewe, thrust, crash, strike)

5

Move one letter from the first word and add it to the second word to make two new words.

Example hunt   sip   <u>hut</u>   <u>snip</u>

56 beacon   snip   _____   _____

57 witch   hair   _____   _____

58 stable   ringing   _____   _____

59 chain   bred   _____   _____

60 night   mean   _____   _____

5

Underline the one word in the brackets which will go with the word outside the brackets in the same way as the first two words go together.

Example good, better   bad, (naughty, worst, <u>worse</u>, nasty)

61 wide, width   high, (height, higher, highest, low)

48

62 tight, loose   short, (small, shrunk, tall, even)

63 hottest, hotter   least, (less, hot, lesser, lesson)

64 tops, spot   part, (past, trap, rapt, step)

65 calm, palm   cane, (pare, pane, care, cape)   **5**

Underline the two words in each line which are made from the same letters.

Example   TAP   PET   <u>TEA</u>   POT   <u>EAT</u>

66 PARADE   DEARER   LAMENT   MENTAL   PARENT

67 REPORT   PORTER   TREATS   STREET   STRIPE

68 UGLIER   GRUELS   DRIEST   STRIDE   GUESTS

69 LATENT   TALENT   STALER   RESTED   TRUEST

70 LEADER   DREAMS   SMEARED   INDEED   DEALER   **5**

Change the first word into the last word, by changing one letter at a time and making a new, different word in the middle.

Example   CASE   <u>CASH</u>   LASH

71 YARD   _____   HAND

72 TAPE   _____   TALK

73 FISH   _____   DASH

74 COMB   _____   CORE

75 DEAF   _____   READ   **5**

The code for BREAK is A S D B J. Use this code to answer the following questions.

76 Which of these codes is the right one for CAVES: B B U F R or B B W D T? _____

77 Which of these words is the right one for R U D F O: STEEP or STEER? _____

78 Which of these codes is the right one for GRAIN: F S Z J M or F S Z J O? _____

79 Which of these words is the right one for R U Z M K: STALK or STALL?

_____

80 Which of these codes is the right one for FUZZY: E V Y Y X or E V Y A X? _____

5

Find the four-letter word hidden in each sentence. Each begins at the end of one word and the beginning of another word, and can cover two or three words. The order of the letters may not be changed.

Example   We had bat<u>s and</u> balls. <u>sand</u>

81 To tremendous applause, the young players ran onto the pitch. _____

82 We apologised when we broke the glass in the classroom window next to the playground. _____

83 I counted three large fish swimming slowly round the pond. _____

84 After working for a long time in the baking sun, we had a break. _____

85 Please leave the door to the church open, when you leave. _____

5

Now go to the Progress Chart to record your score!   Total   85

Mixed paper 7

Change the first word of the third pair in the same way as the other pairs to give a new word.

Example   bind, hind   bare, hare   but, <u>hut</u>

1 great, grate   fear, fare   steal, _____

2 drum, dam   begin, ban   closet, _____

3 bend, bent   form, fort   trail, _____

4 beam, me   mesh, he   cost, _____

5 dust, stud   dame, mead   much, _____

5

Underline the one word in the brackets which will go equally well with both sets of words outside the brackets.

Example   rush, attack   cost, fee   (price, hasten, strike, <u>charge</u>, money)

6 road, path	method, style	(track, way, route, distance, manner)
7 pale, faint	lamp, lantern	(torch, soft, gentle, light, candle)
8 long for, miss	evergreen tree	(fir, yew, pine, yearn, ache)
9 slapdash, lax	limp, loose	(sagging, slack, slow, negligent, careless)
10 air movement	twist, turn	(current, air, wind, loop, snake)
11 excellent, very good	enormous, vast	(large, huge, great, wonderful, fat)
12 unripe, grassy	a colour	(green, blue, yellow, apple, white)
13 sphere, game component	dance, smart party	(cone, rule, ball, disco, game)

Fill in the crosswords so that all the given words are included. You have been given one letter as a clue in each crossword.

14

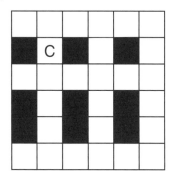

PICKLE TOKENS TIPTOE

FEISTY ENERGY ICICLE

15

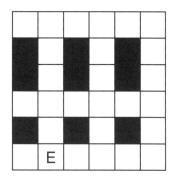

PRAYER RATTLE SEASON

REASON YOUTHS STATUS

If the code for GARAGE is H Z S Z H D, match the right word to each code given below.

SAND   HAND   HARD   DASH

16 I Z O C   _____   18 E Z T G   _____

17 I Z S C   _____   19 T Z O C   _____

20 Using the same code, what is the code for RASH? _____ 5

Change the first word into the last word, by changing one letter at a time and making two new, different words in the middle.

Example CASE	<u>CASH</u>	<u>WASH</u>	WISH
21 TAPE	_____	_____	TOLL
22 GIFT	_____	_____	RAPT
23 SHOD	_____	_____	FLOW
24 SLUR	_____	_____	SPIN
25 RAGE	_____	_____	HIVE

5

Underline the pair of words which are the most similar in meaning.

Example come, go	<u>roams, wanders</u>	fear, fare
26 bare, naked	clip, short	hold, touch
27 encourage, debate	climb, ascend	high, low
28 time, minute	clock, speed	steal, rob
29 halo, angel	pig, hog	yellow, white
30 pardon, forgive	carry, drop	above, below

5

Find the two missing pairs of letters in the following sequences.

A B C D E F G H I J K L M N O P Q R S T U V W X Y Z

Example CQ	DP	EQ	FP	<u>GQ</u>	<u>HP</u>
31 __	HG	__	LI	NJ	PK
32 XA	YC	__	AG	__	CK
33 __	__	TZ	KY	TX	KW
34 DR	BU	__	__	VD	TG
35 VE	WD	XC	YB	__	__

5

Find a word that can be put either in front or at the end of each of the following words to make new, compound words.

Example cast   fall   ward   pour   <u>down</u>

36 free	less	taker	worn	_____
37 bid	give	got	mat	_____
38 hold	break	wife	keeper	_____
39 ridge	wheel	on	horse	_____
40 end	room	work	ally	_____	5

41 If the code for CRATE is F U D W H, what is the code for BOXES?

_____

42 If the code for MOUTH is N N V S I, what is the code for NOSES?

_____

43 If the code for CHILD is E G K K F, what does I H T K U stand for?

_____

44 If the code for HOUSE is E L R P B, what does S F I I X stand for?

_____

45 If the code for BERRY is F I V V C, what does W X V E A stand for?

_____ 5

STORK   SWALLOW   SWIFT   SPARROW   STARLING

If these birds are put into alphabetical order, which comes:

46 third? _____   **47** fifth? _____

If the letters of the word BREAKING are put into alphabetical order, which comes:

48 first? _____   **50** fourth? _____   **49** seventh? _____ 5

Find the four-letter word which can be added to the letters in capitals to make a new word. The new word will complete the sentence sensibly.

Example   They enjoyed the BCAST. <u>ROAD</u>

51 Matt scored fifty runs in the CET match at school. _____

52 Supper's ready; so please lay the T! _____

53 Mary SL her birthday cake into twelve pieces with a sharp knife.

_____

54 Although he slammed on the BS, Aidan's bike crashed into the wall.

_____

55 Our garden H badly needs clipping. _____ 5

Find the four-letter word hidden at the end of one word and the beginning of the next word. The order of the letters may not be changed.

Example We had ba<u>ts and</u> balls. <u>sand</u>

56 We went by bus to the Houses of Parliament. _____

57 Sixty six divided by sixty six equals one. _____

58 We need to collect our tickets from the bus station. _____

59 The trees by the lake dropped their leaves into the murky water.

_____

60 Our school dinner lady is friendly and helpful. _____

5

Underline the one word in the brackets which will go with the word outside the brackets in the same way as the first two words go together.

Example good, better   bad, (naughty, worst, <u>worse</u>, nasty)

61 lift, raise   sustain, (support, carry, elevate, meet)

62 finger, toe   hand, (nail, digit, arm, foot)

63 melon, lemon   mites, (mates, stamp, times, smite)

64 cat, claw   person, (foot, toenail, heel, toe)

65 gnome, game   chose, (case, hose, cosy, chase)

5

If the letters of the word FLAMINGO are put into alphabetical order, which comes:

66 second? _____   67 fifth? _____   68 eighth? _____

If the letters of the word SECONDLY are put into alphabetical order, which comes:

69 third? _____   70 sixth? _____

5

Find the two letters that will end the first word and start the second word.

Example pas (<u>ta</u>) ste

71 you (__ __) an   74 ar (__ __) rth

72 fl (__ __) it   75 op (__ __) low

73 brui (__ __) al

5

Find the missing letters. The alphabet has been written out to help you.

A B C D E F G H I J K L M N O P Q R S T U V W X Y Z

Example AB is to CD as PQ is to <u>RS</u>.

76 UT is to SR as ZY is to __.   79 BB to EF as JJ is to __.

77 FA is to GB as HC is to __.   80 GT is to HS as IR is to __.

78 MN is to LO as FG is to __.

⬤ 5

Look at the first group of three words. The word in the middle has been made from the two other words. Complete the second group of three words in the same way, making a new word in the middle.

Example PAIN	INTO	T<u>OO</u>K	ALSO	<u>SOON</u>	ONLY
81 HARE	LAKE	LOOK	BONE	_____	NEED
82 VASE	VAST	VENT	SALT	_____	FAZE
83 QUIZ	PILE	PLEA	THIN	_____	STEW
84 CORN	CORE	CASE	FROM	_____	WING
85 TIME	MATE	CALM	CASH	_____	BUSH

⬤ 5

Now go to the Progress Chart to record your score!   Total ⬤ 85

Mixed paper 8

1 If the code for GLASS is H K B R T, what is the code for WATER?

_____

2 If the code for SPRAY is Q N P Y W, what does F M Q C Q stand for?

_____

3 If the code for GREEN is I T G G P, what does D N C E M stand for?

_____

4 If the code for LAMPS is J C K R Q, what is the code for SHADE?

_____

5 If the code for RIVER is S J W F S, what is the code for FLOOD?

_____

⬤ 5

Underline the one word in the brackets which will go equally well with both sets of words outside the brackets.

Example rush, attack   cost, fee   (price, hasten, strike, <u>charge</u>, money)

6 bird limb   sport position   (leg, centre, half, wing, forearm)

7 terrible, tragic   a colour   (blue, grim, fateful, black, indigo)

8 animal skin   conceal, shroud   (leather, hide, camouflage, fur, cloak)

9 fastener, bar   run away or eat quickly   (gobble, escape, bolt, flee, gorge)

10 vital, critical   lock opener   (crucial, decisive, key, jemmy, bar)   5

Change the first word into the last word, by changing one letter at a time and making two new, different words in the middle.

Example CASE   <u>CASH</u>   <u>WASH</u>   WISH

11 SAME   _____   _____   FUSE

12 TWIG   _____   _____   CHIN

13 BASH   _____   _____   WITH

14 FACT   _____   _____   WADE

15 MOOD   _____   _____   NOUN   5

Find the missing letters. The alphabet has been written out to help you.

A B C D E F G H I J K L M N O P Q R S T U V W X Y Z

Example AB is to CD as PQ is to <u>RS</u>.

16 KL is to IJ as FG is to __.   19 SU is to QW as XZ is to __.

17 AZ is to BY as CX is to __.   20 TY is to UZ as VA is to __.

18 AF is to CG as BG is to __.   5

21 If the code for CROWN is D Q P V O, what is the code for QUEEN?

_____

22 If the code for GRAPE is I T C R G, what is the code for FRUIT?

_____

23 If the code for SHIRT is O D E N P, what does F A W J O stand for?

_____

24 If the code for ARROW is Y S P P U, what is the code for SWORD?

_____

25 If the code for SMALL is U L C K N, what does N Z T F G stand for?

_____

Change the first word of the third pair in the same way as the other pairs to give a new word.

Example bind, hind   bare, hare   but, <u>hut</u>

26 scrape, cap   cheats, hat   barter, _____

27 calm, lame   port, rote   film, _____

28 best, bees   felt, feel   kept, _____

29 swan, sawn   blot, bolt   silt, _____

30 churches, chest   larkspur, spurt   undercover, _____

Underline the one word in the brackets which will go with the word outside the brackets in the same way as the first two words go together.

Example good, better   bad, (naughty, worst, <u>worse</u>, nasty)

31 clear, cloudy   still, (almost, sparkling, gloomy, motionless)

32 battle, fight   game, (football, play, run, think, avoid)

33 plain, patterned   flat, (house, striped, brick, uneven)

34 cut, bleed   bump, (bruise, ramp, water, leg)

35 plump, pup   crust, (rust, rut, cut, cur)

Look at the first group of three words. The word in the middle has been made from the two other words. Complete the second group of three words in the same way, making a new word in the middle.

Example PAIN   INTO   T<u>OO</u>K   ALSO   <u>SOON</u>   ONLY

36 CAME   MEAT   BATH   BOOM   _____   BENT

37 BACK   JACK   JURY   DEEP   _____   WING

38 BENT   DENT   DIRT   BEST   _____   VAIN

| 39 | HARM | MARK | KERB | BOAT | _____ | BOMB |
| 40 | KISS | SHIP | HOPE | PINK | _____ | AXLE |

5

Find the four-letter word which can be added to the letters in capitals to make a new word. The new word will complete the sentence sensibly.

Example They enjoyed the BCAST. <u>ROAD</u>

41 The racehorses grouped together impatiently, ready to S the race. _____

42 The blue FING light of the ambulance showed up clearly. _____

43 The rugby player wore a red and white STD shirt. _____

44 A tree fell on our house and DAM the roof. _____

45 T pencils you lent me were all blunt! _____

5

Find the four-letter word hidden at the end of one word and the beginning of the next word. The order of the letters may not be changed.

Example We had bat<u>s and</u> balls. <u>sand</u>

46 Your skull protects your brain from harm. _____

47 I think those exhibition pictures are colourful and attractive. _____

48 A fox chased a baby rabbit and scared her badly. _____

49 Why are stamps so expensive now? _____

50 The nurse put a plaster cast on his broken arm. _____

5

Find the two missing pairs of letters in the following sequences.

A B C D E F G H I J K L M N O P Q R S T U V W X Y Z

Example	CQ	DP	EQ	FP	<u>GQ</u>	<u>HP</u>
51	ZZ	__	VV	__	RR	PP
52	__	LN	MM	__	MK	LJ
53	AD	GJ	__	SV	__	EH
54	__	WV	ZS	CP	FM	__
55	MD	__	WZ	BX	__	LT

5

Underline the pair of words which are the most similar in meaning.

Example come, go   <u>roams, wanders</u>   fear, fare

56 bed, window   chair, sofa   table, cupboard

57 red, green   blue, orange   purple, violet

58 leopard, lion   monkey, bear   fish, bird

59 kind, sort   hold, drop   behind, above

60 right, left   gesture, signal   both, together   **5**

If the letters of the word BRIGHTEN are put into alphabetical order, which comes:

61 sixth? _____   **62** fourth? _____   **63** eighth? _____

GREEN   BLUE   BLACK   BROWN   GREY

If these colours are put in alphabetical order, which comes:

64 first? _____   **65** fifth? _____   **5**

At a summer camp, five children wore either blue, green or red shorts and either red, blue or green shirts.

Two children wore red shorts, two wore blue shorts and one wore green.

Two children wore green shirts, two wore blue shirts and one wore red.

John wore blue shorts and shirt. He was the only one to wear one colour.

Leena wore red shorts and Sam wore a blue shirt.

Sarah had one colour in common with Leena.

Micah wore green shorts.

From the information, work out which child wore which clothes and answer the questions.

66 What colour was Micah's shirt?_____

67 What was the colour Sarah had in common with Leena? _____

68 Who wore the red shirt? _____

69 Who, besides John, wore blue shorts? _____

70 Who wore red shorts and a blue shirt? _____   **5**

Find the two letters that will end the first word and start the second word.

Example pas (ta) ste

71 be (__ __) ch

72 sh (__ __) en

73 mu (__ __) ild

74 mi (__ __) ntre

75 sp (__ __) der

5

Underline the one word in the brackets which will go equally well with each of the words outside the brackets.

Example word, paragraph, sentence   (pen, cap, <u>letter</u>, top, stop)

76 feathers, fur, scales   (bird, lizard, cat, skin, fish)

77 comma, full stop, question mark   (sentence, page, speech, apostrophe, number)

78 metre, hectare, kilogram   (weight, height, length, mass, centimetre)

79 roll, loaf, bap   (cake, hot dog, bread, slice, cupcake)

80 steel, iron, tin   (can, metal, diamond, spoon, stainless)

5

Find a word that can be put either in front or at the end of each of the following words to make new, compound words.

Example cast   fall   ward   pour   <u>down</u>

81 grey   blood   fox   wolf   _____

82 jumping   ground   down   case   _____

83 burn   line   ways   step   _____

84 back   able   phone   roll   _____

85 chair   fire   post   sports   _____

5

QUALIT Y
AT WORK

DIANE BONE and RICK GRIGGS

KOGAN
PAGE

Acknowledgements

We wish to thank the following people for their valuable contributions to this book. Their support has added depth and breadth to the content of the book and enriched our lives. These individuals have proved by example that quality at work, works!

John Asquith, Catherine Ayers, Dave Burgett, Ed Diehl, Rick Gilbert, Patricia Goelzer, Richard Gordon, Jon Green, Walt Hurd, Patricia Lowell, Wendy Coleman Lucas, Joe Shea, Terry Stamps and Greg Swartz.

First published in the United States of America
in 1989 by Crisp Publications Inc, 95 First Street,
Los Altos, California 94022, USA.

This edition first published in Great Britain in
1989 by Kogan Page Ltd, 120 Pentonville Road,
London N1 9JN.

British Library Cataloguing in Publication Data
Bone, Diane
  Quality at work.
  1. Industries. Quality control
  I. Title   II. Griggs, Rick
  658.5'62

  ISBN 0-7494-0033-1
  ISBN 0-7494-0034-X pbk

Typeset by DP Photosetting, Aylesbury, Bucks
Printed and bound in Great Britain by
Biddles Ltd, Guildford

QUALITY AT WORK

◀ CONTENTS ▶

Acknowledgements   4

Preface   9

About This Book   11

1. Quality Consciousness   13
    Quality consciousness checklist *13*
    Where there's smoke ... *15*
    The 'No Worse' trap *16*
    What quality is and is not *17*
    Why worry about quality? *18*
    Twenty reasons to adopt a quality programme *18*
    The challenge of quality *19*

2. Personal Quality Standards   21
    Notice your personal standards *22*
    Preparing to develop personal standards *23*
    My personal standards *25*
    Is this personal quality? You decide! *26*

Lighting the Quality MATCH *28*
The Q-MATCH Test *29*
Where can I apply Q-MATCH? *30*
Quality and expectations *30*
P-A-S Options for quality *31*
Personal standard measurement form *32*
What makes us compromise (cheat)? *33*

3. The Three Cs of Quality   **36**
Commitment *37*
Competence *39*
Communication *40*
Authors' comments *43*
Suggestions for communicating quality *44*

4. Your Organisation's Goals   **45**
Your mission role *46*
Check your goal control *46*
Setting quality standards *47*
What's wrong with this story? *48*

5. PS: The Perfection Standard   **50**
PS (Perfection Standards) *51*
Putting PS to work: 'Just do it!' *52*
The Seven-Step Plan: a preview *52*
The Seven-Step Plan for measuring quality performance *53*
An action-orientated quality plan *57*

6. The 'How-To' of Quality   **59**
1. Identify and solve quality problems *60*
2. Ensure customer satisfaction *63*
3. Measure results *65*

4. Reward quality performance *68*

5. Set up quality groups *68*

6. Provide quality training *73*

7. Assess the cost of quality *76*

8. Establish your quality programme *79*

9. Support your quality programme *80*

10. Make quality work *83*

7. A Mention of Prevention   **84**
Principles of prevention *85*
How to prevent errors *86*
Prevention v Correction *87*

8. Quality Beginning to End: A Review   **88**

Glossary   **91**

Bibliography   **94**

◀ PREFACE ▶

Quality is a standard by which we judge our work. It measures whether we did what we set out to do and is the standard by which customers measure products or services. To establish quality guidelines, we must have a starting point and some no-nonsense criteria. A quality programme must also be fun and rewarding to get enthusiastic support. *Quality at Work* makes a breakthrough by presenting the basics of quality in an easy-to-understand format designed to help management and employees to establish and meet simple, effective quality standards.

This book is for everyone who works. As an employee, you make a significant contribution to your organisation by bringing high personal standards to your job. This book helps you to examine the role of quality in your life and work.

If you are a supervisor or manager, you will find step-by-step guidance and a clear definition of quality. You alone provide the leadership and support needed for a strong quality programme. *Quality at Work* helps you and your colleagues to set realistic standards for departmental and organisational goals.

Quality at Work is about personal and job-related quality. Chapters 1 to 3 help the reader to identify the personal quality standards and goals that support their quality standards at work. Chapters 4 to 7 relate more closely to work issues.

Chapter 1 defines quality, provides examples of quality and tells why it is important. Quality begins with the individual, and in Chapter 2 you have the opportunity to assess your individual standards of quality. How were they developed? Why are they important? How do they relate to your work? Chapter 3 discusses the intangibles of quality – commitment, competence and communication. In order to establish quality standards we must know the purpose of our individual jobs and the work of our organisation.

Chapter 4 identifies organisational goals and gives guidelines for setting quality goals based on our work purpose. In Chapter 5 you will find a Seven-Step Plan that you and your department can use to establish Perfection Standards (PS) to determine what quality work is. (What is quality for one job or service may not be quality for another. An industrial diamond does not have to be as nearly perfect as one that will be used as a setting in fine jewellery. Quality depends on purpose.)

Chapter 6, the 'How To' chapter, provides valuable guidelines on quality issues, including problem solving, customer satisfaction, measuring results, rewarding quality performance, setting up quality groups, providing training, assessing the cost of quality, establishing a quality programme and supporting your quality programme. Chapter 7 discusses error prevention and supports the concept of doing the job right the first time.

This book is for people concerned about quality. Of course, no one is against quality, but implementing personal and work-related guidelines can be frustrating. *Quality at Work* answers the question: 'How can we set quality standards that are personally satisfying and help our organisation to do what we say we will do when we say we will do it, in a way that meets our customers' needs?'

If quality is your goal, we can help. We hope you enjoy using our material. Turn the page and let's get started.

Diane Bone
Rick Griggs

◀ ABOUT THIS BOOK ▶

Quality at Work is not like most books. It stands out from other self-help books in an important way. It's not a book to read – it's a book to *use*. The unique 'self-paced' format of this book, and its many worksheets, encourage the reader to get involved and try some new ideas immediately.

Using the simple yet sound techniques presented will help the reader to understand what quality means and why personal standards of quality are essential for success both in your career and in your life.

Quality at Work (and other self-improvement titles listed on page 94) can be used effectively in a number of ways. Here are some possibilities:

Individual study. Because the book is self-instructional, all that is needed is a quiet place, some time and a pencil. By completing the activities and exercises, a reader should receive not only valuable feedback but also practical steps for self-improvement.

Workshops and seminars. This book is ideal for assigned reading prior to a workshop or seminar. With the basics in hand, the quality of the participation will improve. The book is also effective when it is distributed at the beginning of a session and participants work through the contents.

Open learning. Books can be sent to those unable to attend training sessions.

There are several other possibilities that depend on the objective, programme or ideas of the user.

One thing is certain, even after it has been read, this book will be looked at – and thought about – again and again.

◀ CHAPTER 1 ▶

QUALITY CONSCIOUSNESS

'There is no limit to the quality that can be produced, even in the most menial job.'

Dave Thomas

Quality is a perfection standard to be practised at all times; it is a continual effort to improve.

Quality is a standard, a goal or a set of requirements. Quality is a measurable goal, not a vague sense of goodness. It is a continual effort to improve rather than a set degree of excellence. It is a result. We cannot possess quality, we can only practise it. *Quality is a perfection standard by which we decide whether we did what we set out to do when and how we said we would do it, in a way that meets our customers' needs.* Were our customers happy with the way we provided our service or made our widgets? If so, we can say we met our quality goals.

Dr J M Juran says that manufacturing quality is 'fitness for purpose'. In service industries which are somewhat subjective, we say that a quality service is one that is 'fit to be tried'. In other words, employees have agreed to try quality practices and measure quality results through customer feedback. An A+ report card from internal and external customers is the final test of quality.

Quality consciousness checklist

Quality begins with awareness. You probably developed an early 'quality consciousness' as a consumer. Remember how you liked the mint-green toothpaste better than the white kind? Later you made many life choices based on quality: where you lived and worked, who

Raise your consciousness about quality.

13

your friends were, what lifestyle you wanted. Consider each of the following statements and mark it true or false based on your current awareness of quality at work and in your personal life. See the authors' comments on the next page.

True   **False**

____   ____   1. Quality is preventing problems rather than picking up the pieces afterwards.

____   ____   2. Quality can always be improved.

____   ____   3. The KISS (Keep It Simple, Stupid!) method is the best way to ensure quality.

____   ____   4. The most important reason for a quality programme at work is to have satisfied customers.

____   ____   5. Constant attention to quality is unnecessary.

____   ____   6. First impressions aren't important in creating a quality environment.

____   ____   7. Quality is the little things as well as the big things.

____   ____   8. A quality programme must have management support to be successful.

____   ____   9. Quality guidelines are best communicated by word of mouth.

____   ____   10. Most people want to do quality work.

____   ____   11. Customers pay little attention to quality.

____   ____   12. A quality programme must mesh with the organisation's goals and profit plans.

____   ____   13. Quality means conformity to standards.

____   ____   14. Quality should operate in all parts of a business.

____   ____   15. Personal quality standards and business quality standards have little in common.

____   ____   16. Quality requires commitment.

____   ____   17. Quality relates to the process as much as to the goal.

____   ____   18. People who talk about quality are idealists.

Where there's smoke ...

Imagine what would happen if an emergency service neglected to attend to issues of quality. The following scene illustrates how much we are dependent on professionals in the public sector to make quality a high priority.

The warning bell in the Farmer Street Fire Station sounds abrasively as Patrick shakes himself awake. It is 3.00 am and a two-alarm fire is burning out of control in a vacant warehouse a mile away. The on-duty fire crew slowly pull themselves from their warm bunks and fumble for their coats and boots. 'Where are my gloves?' wonders Patrick as he saunters towards Engine No 1. Recently he noticed that the old truck had been given to spells of battery failure. 'Should report that,' thought Patrick idly.

Patrick gives a final wrap to secure a water hose on the truck. A loose nozzle falls from the attached hose and clatters to the floor. 'Should fix that,' he mutters, as he climbs into the cab and yells for everyone to climb aboard. The crew grumble as they climb on the tail board. Joe, the trainee, is nowhere to be seen.

'Hey, Joe, let's go!' yells Patrick. Joe appears, looking sleepy and confused. 'I thought this was another false alarm,' he says.

'Get on, Joe, this is the real thing,' yells Patrick, slightly annoyed. Patrick cranks the key on the big red engine and the engine grinds hesitantly, then dies. 'Should get this fixed,' Patrick

A negligent approach can be disastrous.

Answers. 1.–4. T; 5. F (Quality does not take care of itself. It takes time, energy and creativity to maintain a successful quality programme.) **6. F** (The first impression may be the only chance to sell an idea, service or product. Quality is important down to the smallest detail, and it has to be right – the first time.) **7. T, 8. T, 9. F** (Quality guidelines must be issued officially from the top and they must be in writing. They should also be agreed to by employees.) **10. T, 11. F** (Customers today are sophisticated and demanding, and pay as much attention to quality as to price.) **12.–14. T, 15. F** (Personal and business quality standards are inseparable. People with high personal standards will be the ones to lead business quality programmes.) **16.–17. T, 18. F** (People who talk about quality are realists. The only way to compete successfully today is continually to improve quality.)

growls. 'All out, everyone, battery trouble. Unload and reload on Engine No 2.'

Engine No 2 swings slowly from the fire station. Joe hangs precariously from the safety bar scratching his head. 'I really thought this was a false alarm.'

Analyse the example

Had this story been true, what were the crew's chances of getting to the fire before the building was destroyed? In your opinion, what quality problems did the Farmer Street Fire Station have? Tick your responses on the list below.

☐ No clear guidelines for quality standards

☐ Poor maintenance

☐ Poor team spirit

☐ Inadequate training

☐ No sense of urgency

☐ Lack of communication

☐ Unconcerned leadership

☐ No preventive thinking

Others _____

If you ticked all of them, you're right! Fortunately, the Farmer Street Fire Station doesn't exist. However, their problems *do* exist in many businesses because they are not yet quality conscious. They need to understand quality and why it is important to adopt a quality programme.

The 'No Worse' trap

In *Passion for Excellence,** Tom Peters tells this startling story:

'Quality is about passion and pride.'

Quality is about passion and pride. Sometime back Tom spent two days in a series of seminars with managers of a major retail chain. In the course of the meeting the subject of affordable levels of

---

* *Passion for Excellence*, Thomas Peters and Nancy Austin, Collins, London, 1985.

service came up continually. At one point Tom was well launched on a bit of a diatribe about the rotten level of service in retailing in general when an executive vice president, in front of forty of his peers and subordinates, got up and interrupted him: 'Tom, sit down and calm down. Or get off our case. It's a changing and complex and highly competitive world. *We are no worse than anybody else.*'

To avoid the 'No Worse' trap, individuals and organisations need to look realistically at quality. It is not an impossible dream: it is an everyday reality practised by thousands of people and organisations who see the pay-off for setting standards and living up to them.

Quality is not an impossible dream; it is a reality practised by many people and organisations.

What quality is and is not

Here is a list of attributes describing what quality is and is not. Use this list to identify your personal and professional responses to the quality challenge. Add your own ideas at the bottom.

Quality is	Quality is not
A philosophy	A quick fix
Conformity to perfection standards	Goodness
Prevention	Merely inspection
Following specific guidelines	A 'close enough' attitude
A lifelong process	A motivational programme
Commitment	Coincidence
Supported by upper management	Randomly adopted
A positive attitude	A watchdog mentality
Agreement	Doing your own thing
Willing communication	Isolated data
Understanding your processes	Guessing
Identifying opportunities for error	Detecting errors in end products
Add your own:	Add your own:
_____	_____
_____	_____
_____	_____

Definition of quality.

Why worry about quality?

Benefits to the organisation of a quality programme.

Why should our organisation develop a quality consciousness? Why should we adopt a quality programme? What are the advantages of moving from a random method of 'putting out fires' to a preventive, planned system for delivering quality goods and services? List as many reasons as you can think of in the space below. Place a ☑ next to those that are most important to you. Then continue below and read 'Twenty reasons to adopt a quality programme.' Tick any you would like to add to your list.

Reasons to adopt a quality programme

Important
to me

☐ _____

☐ _____

☐ _____

☐ _____

☐ _____

☐ _____

☐ _____

Twenty reasons to adopt a quality programme

Important
to me

☐ 1. To be profitable

☐ 2. To be 'recession proof'

☐ 3. To enjoy the results

☐ 4. To reinforce personal quality standards

☐ 5. To maintain customer confidence

☐ 6. To build customer loyalty

☐ 7. To improve customer satisfaction

☐   8. To maintain corporate vitality

☐   9. To use employees' creative energies

☐   10. To develop a good reputation

☐   11. To promote human dignity

☐   12. To lower costs

☐   13. To retain employees

☐   14. To increase productivity

☐   15. To contribute to society

☐   16. To create a clear vision of the organisation

☐   17. To improve technology

☐   18. To solve problems effectively

☐   19. To increase competitiveness

☐   20. To develop internal cooperation

Add your own:

☐ _____

☐ _____

☐ _____

The challenge of quality

Quality is an elusive goal. Once you have produced a quality product or service, you must sustain and improve that level. Quality is a moving target. Your competition improves, customers evolve and demand changes, and supplies become scarce. Tick the suggestions that you think will help you to meet your personal and professional quality goals.

Quality is a moving target. Once produced, it has to be sustained.

☐   Learn all you can about quality.

☐   Apply quality standards to appropriate work issues.

☐   Blame others when quality wavers.

☐   Work with others in accomplishing your quality goals.

☐ Don't worry about a little inconsistency.

☐ Know how your quality goals relate to your organisation's mission.

List below some quality challenges in your work or your personal life and list one or two solutions that will help you to meet them.

	Challenge	**Solution(s)**
1.	_____	_____
		_____
2.	_____	_____
		_____
3.	_____	_____
		_____
4.	_____	_____
		_____
5.	_____	_____
		_____

◄ CHAPTER 2 ►

PERSONAL QUALITY STANDARDS

'Quality involves living the message of the possibility of perfection and infinite improvement, living it day in and day out, decade by decade.'

Thomas Peters

Your personal quality standards are what make you say, 'That waitress is doing a good job!' These same standards cause you to think, 'If I get service this bad again at the counter, I'll never come back!'

Personal standards of quality are applied all the time.

Everywhere you drive, each time you buy your lunch, and every time you make a purchase, you are applying your personal standards of quality. We all make quick judgements about the workers at the side of the road: some do an excellent job, while others just sit. We tell our colleagues that the service at the new lunch bar is terrible, but the roast beef is delicious. And each time we buy stockings, shirts, shoes or jewellery we evaluate the way we're treated by the sales assistant.

In all these cases, we're using our personal standards for quality to assess whether other people are doing what they said they would do, when they said they would do it.

Definition

Personal quality standards are the acid tests we use on ourselves and others to see if we act and perform the way we said (or implied) we would act.

Albert Einstein said that 'Whoever is careless with the truth in small matters cannot be trusted with important matters.' This can be scary. At first glance, we might think that every little thing in our lives is extremely important and that every detail must be perfect. How can you keep track of everything and still do it to the highest level of performance? The answer is: *Pick your battles and then perform as agreed.*

Work on your own personal standards.

See what you think of the following personal quality standards. Take a look at the subject or topic of the standard and also the *level of performance* attached to each one. Compare these standards with your own, and tick whether yours are the same, higher or lower.

My standards are:

Higher Same Lower

☐ ☐ ☐ 1. Get to all appointments within *5 minutes* of the agreed time.

☐ ☐ ☐ 2. *Never* criticise family members in front of outsiders.

☐ ☐ ☐ 3. Stay within *10 miles* of the speed limit.

☐ ☐ ☐ 4. *Never* speed in school zones or near children.

☐ ☐ ☐ 5. Exercise at least *twice a week.*

☐ ☐ ☐ 6. Wear *only* neat, clean clothing outside the house.

☐ ☐ ☐ 7. Write cheques no more than *one day* before depositing the money.

☐ ☐ ☐ 8. Return phone calls within *one hour* of receiving the message.

☐ ☐ ☐ 9. Flirt *occasionally* with attractive men/women in *social situations.*

Notice your personal standards

Assess your personal standards.

You may have noticed that some of these personal quality standards make you feel uncomfortable. You have already compared them with your own personal expectations *and* you've made a judgement about whether they're too strict or too lenient.

If your personal standards are rather strict, you may have thought:

- Ten miles above the speed limit is illegal and I wouldn't do it.
- Exercising only twice a week isn't good enough for cardiovascular fitness.
- How could someone *think* of writing a cheque *before* depositing the money?
- You should never flirt!

If your personal standards do not focus on these areas, you may have thought:

- I go 20 miles above the speed limit (and I've never had an accident!).
- Exercising twice a month is more than enough (you could kill yourself!).
- If a cheque bounces, they can send it through again … I'm not a crook!
- Romance is the spice of life! There's nothing wrong with it, even at work.

Preparing to develop personal standards

A. List the different areas of your life

This may seem strange at first: name all the areas that are important to you in your personal life. Examples: Health, Family, Hobbies, Finances, Leisure, Travel, Growth, Relationships, Career, Education, Reading, Writing.

Learn to develop your personal standards.

_____ _____ _____ _____

_____ _____ _____ _____

_____ _____ _____ _____

B. Prioritise the areas of your life

Putting them in order will attach a priority to each segment of your personal life. You may choose to focus only on certain areas.

1st_____ 2nd_____ 3rd_____ 4th_____

5th_____ 6th_____ 7th_____ 8th_____

9th_____ 10th_____ 11th_____ 12th_____

C. List the goal or end result

Now imagine how your life will look when the top 4 to 5 priority areas are fully developed. Some of your personal areas will have values attached (for example, Honesty, Loyalty, Trust). Examples of goals: 1st = Honest/open family communications. 2nd = Healthy/fit body. 3rd = New career paths.

	Life area	End result/Goal
1st	_____	_____
2nd	_____	_____
3rd	_____	_____
4th	_____	_____
5th	_____	_____

D. Describe specific activities to reach each goal

Work to reach your goals.

These are the steps you take to reach end results. In other words, list the means to the end. In cases where no specific end result is targeted, the process or the means is most important.

Remember: The goal is the *end result*, and the activities are what you get there.

Example: 1st goal: *Receive my degree.*

Activities: (a) *Sign on for classes.* (b) *Attend classes.* (c) *Pass exams.*

1st goal: _____

Activities: (a) _____ (b) _____ (c) _____

2nd goal: _____

Activities: (a) _____ (b) _____ (c) _____

3rd goal: _____

Activities: (a) _____ (b) _____ (c) _____

4th goal: _____

Activities: (a) ——————— (b) ——————— (c) ———————

5th goal: ————————————————————————————————

Activities: (a) ——————— (b) ——————— (c) ———————

My personal standards

'I don't believe in setting up universal standards that a large proportion of people can't reach.'

Margaret Mead

Write down your initial ideas for personal standards. Don't worry about whether they are perfectly thought out or well written. Just jot down some areas you feel are important and how strict you want to be in each area. *Base these standards on the goals and activities you listed as important to you in the last few pages. Ignore the P-A-S Options column.* You'll fill it in when you reach page 32.

Standards that are important to you.

Examples: A. Never miss more than one class session per term.
B. Receive at least average pass marks on all tests.

P-A-S Options

	P	A	S
1. ————————————————	☐	☐	☐
2. ————————————————	☐	☐	☐
3. ————————————————	☐	☐	☐
4. ————————————————	☐	☐	☐
5. ————————————————	☐	☐	☐
6. ————————————————	☐	☐	☐
7. ————————————————	☐	☐	☐
8. ————————————————	☐	☐	☐
9. ————————————————	☐	☐	☐
10. ————————————————	☐	☐	☐

You'll find that you actually do have standards in your personal life and an idea of how strictly you feel they should be observed.

Before discussing the level of quality for each standard, let's take a look at some examples of personal standards and a quick 'acid test' for measuring quality. We'll come back to this page later.

Is this personal quality? You decide!

Other people's personal standards.

James drives into a clean and apparently efficient service station to fill up. As he drives in he sees a woman pull out, so he takes the same unleaded pump she has just used.

There's no one around, so he steps over a large puddle of water and starts pumping. When the tank is half full, an attendant casually walks up and says, 'Hey, you'd better be careful. That puddle you're standing in isn't water ... it's petrol. The hose broke on a lady a while ago ... you should've seen the petrol spurting out!'

James asks, 'Well, why don't you clean it up? Customers don't expect to come here and step in petrol!' The attendant replies, 'Ah, it'll evaporate. That'll be £15 for your fill-up, sir.'

What do you think about:

This attendant's personal standards? _____

Is quality an issue here? _____

What would your standard be? _____

Martin works in a high-rise building. His window used to overlook a park and an old office building. The office building was torn down to build the new Town Hall and leisure centre. Martin is fascinated as he watches the daily progress. He is also surprised at some of the things the workers do right in front of his 12-storey building, where dozens of people could be watching!

Scene 1. Martin looks up from his computer and can't believe what he sees. There's a worker taking off his trousers in broad daylight! He casually tosses them on to a lorry and grabs his overalls. He then calmly slips into his overalls, totally unaware of 12 storeys of office workers possibly watching him from across the street.

What do you think about:

This person's personal standards? _____

Is quality an issue here? _____

What would your standard be? _____

Scene 2. A few weeks later, Martin sees that the underground parking level is complete, and workers are on the second storey planning to lay concrete. One worker finishes a soft drink, looks around to see if other workers are looking, and then quickly throws the can between two walls of the new building. The can will probably never see light until an excavation team unearths the building in 2000 years' time.

What do you think about:

This person's personal standards? _____

Is quality an issue here? _____

What would your standard be? _____

At the sorting office

Here's a conversation that was overheard at the sorting office. Keep in mind that every large organisation has a variety of people with different standards of quality. Sometimes other people's standards don't match our own or those of the organisation. This does not mean they are good or bad.

This interchange was frustrating to the woman and the person who saw it take place. What do you think of the standards of quality involved?

Woman: *'Good morning. I've come to pick up my parcel. What a long way!'*
Postal Employee: *'Do you have the card we put through your letter box?'*
Woman: *'I think so; let's see ... Oh, here it is ... I'm in a bit of a hurry!'*
Postal Employee: *'Wait here. I'll be back.' (several minutes pass)*
'I'm sorry, we can't find it. Are you sure you haven't already picked it up?'
Woman: *'What? Of course not. I've made a special journey just for this parcel.'*

Postal Employee: *'Well, I'll check again ...' (several more minutes pass) 'Sorry, it's just not here. Are you sure ... oh wait, what's your road number?'*

Woman: *'It's 44.'*

Postal Employee: *'Oh, somebody put it through the wrong door. Sorry!'*

Woman: *'You're joking! I've wasted all this time!'*

Postal Employee: *'I just work here – I don't put the cards through the letter boxes.'*

What do you think about:

This person's personal standards? _____

Is quality an issue here? _____

What would your standard be? _____

Lighting the Quality MATCH

The acid test of quality.

Is there a quick and useful way to compare what you do (and what others do) to some standard? We think there is, and believe it or not, it doesn't have to be complicated. Just remember the quality mnemonic: Q-MATCH which is:

> QUALITY =
>
> **M** EETS
>
> **A** GREED
>
> **T** ERMS and
>
> **CH** ANGES

You could say that Q-MATCH is the light that illuminates the principle of quality. You can apply this acid test to yourself and the important things you do, or to others and the critical tasks they have agreed to perform. The terms and changes are not always plastered across an advertisement in the daily paper. In some cases, terms and changes are just implied, but quality is judged on implications as much as on written contracts.

When you're in these situations ask yourself if the service, performance or activity really **M**eets **A**greed **T**erms and **CH**anges.

- At your bank
- At the department store
- Getting your shoes mended
- Buying a computer
- Getting served at a restaurant
- Getting the newspaper each day
- Repaying a loan
- Borrowing supplies from a colleague
- Showing up for team practice.

The Q-MATCH Test

The acid test: does it Q-MATCH? If it meets agreed terms and changes, it's quality! Remember, although there are different levels of performance, the test is whether it matches what was agreed. Quality at the personal level can mean getting the boy or girl to deliver the paper in the porch *or* specifically to the letter box. Both are quality if they are agreed on. You can also *change* the requirement by asking that the paper is put right through the letter box so it won't get wet or stolen. This new change now defines the performance needed ... in other words the level of quality. Take a look and see if these pass the test:

Apply the Q-MATCH test.

Yes No

1. Your garage mechanic takes two extra days to finish some repairs on your car. **Q-MATCH?**

2. The same mechanic lets you know in advance how long it will take and lends you a car. **Q-MATCH?**

3. Your date or spouse cancels a weekly outing at the last minute. **Q-MATCH?**

4. Your scheduled appointment cancels *again* on the day of the scheduled meeting. **Q-MATCH?**

5. You feel a little ill and decide to skip an appointment and see a film instead. **Q-MATCH?**

6. While jogging, you decide to cut through the car park to save time and effort. **Q-MATCH?**

☐ ☐   7. You've had a final reminder about the gas bill, but it's late on Friday so you wait until Monday to pay. **Q-MATCH?**

☐ ☐   8. You've stopped smoking, but continue to take puffs from friends' cigarettes; that way you're not really smoking. **Q-MATCH?**

☐ ☐   9. Your dentist's appointment is cancelled. They phoned and left a message the day before. **Q-MATCH?**

☐ ☐   10. Your teenage son agrees to clean and wash your car in order to use it tonight. His date is changed to tomorrow night, but the car is still cleaned and washed today. **Q-MATCH?**

Where can I apply Q-MATCH?

Our quality test should be applied to any situation you feel is important. As you get used to using Q-MATCH, you'll find yourself assessing quality performance in an instant.

The Q-MATCH test can help you to ...

- Make purchase decisions
- Negotiate for repairs
- Weigh alternatives for investing
- Decide who to contact on social problems
- Decide who to involve in business matters.

In other words, any time you deal with products, services or activities where you expect certain levels of performance or satisfaction, use the Q-MATCH test to assess quality.

Quality and expectations

Performance standards are measured against the quality received.

A lot of this business of quality boils down to agreed expectations. It's very simple. One party makes a list of what is expected. This might be written, verbal or even a mental note. Another party responds by giving details about which expectations he can and cannot meet. The two parties come to an agreement on what will be delivered and then the delivery is measured against the agreement.

1. Expectations (requirements)
2. Capabilities
3. Agreement (terms, promises, advertisements)
4. Delivery (performance)
5. Measurement.

A story of expectations

Roger manages a department for a medium-sized, high technology firm. His group is responsible for shipping the finished products sold by the marketing department and built by manufacturing. In the past, Roger tried to please everyone in marketing by promising early delivery dates with special last-minute requests. He also wanted to be on good terms with manufacturing, so he didn't complain when production schedules got bogged down and delivery dates were missed. Roger learned the hard way that he couldn't meet everyone's expectations. Marketing, manufacturing and even a few customers made formal complaints about the quality of his department. Today, Roger makes it a policy that everyone in the department follows the five steps mentioned above. They get detailed expectations and then match their capabilities. An agreement is reached to deliver only on the expectations they are capable of meeting. Finally, the performance delivery is measured against the written agreement. Roger doesn't win all the popularity contests but he doesn't get attacked for poor quality either.

P-A-S Options for quality

Quality is not perfection or goodness. Quality at work or at home is meeting expectations. Sometimes it means no mistakes or defects, while at other times less than perfect performance still gives us what we require. Quality means that you **M**eet **A**greed **T**erms and **CH**anges.

Quality means meeting expectations.

P-A-S Options for quality

PERFECTION Option: No mistakes, no defects, inflexible

AVERAGE Option: Past results are fine, very flexible

STRETCH Option: Reasonable difficulty, little flexibility

31

Don't build the habit of failing. Set the right standard from the beginning. Average is appropriate for many situations. Others require the *stretch* or *perfection* options. *Pick the right one at the beginning and obtain an agreement.* This is quality.

Look at the standards you set earlier in the chapter. Go back to page 25 and add P-A-S Options to identify which level of performance would be appropriate.

Measuring personal standards

Measuring your personal goals and standards can only be done by you, because only by using your personal yardstick will you know if you're on the right track. You can measure according to subjective feelings (good or bad), reports from other important people or your sense of satisfaction.

Personal quality standards are measured differently from your standards at work, because they result from your values, attitudes and intuitive judgement. Work standards, on the other hand, must be quantifiable, observable, and results-orientated.

Personal standards	**Work standards**
• values	• quantifiable
• attitudes	• observable
• intuitive judgement	• results orientated

A balanced combination

The personal standard measurement form on page 33 will help you to quantify whether you are meeting your personal standards.

Personal standard measurement form

Meaasuring your own personal standards.

Copy the table for each of your personal standards you listed on page 25. Then circle the number for the way you're currently performing to this standard. Not all measures will apply to each standard. Add any other measures that are important to you.

My personal standard (   ) _____

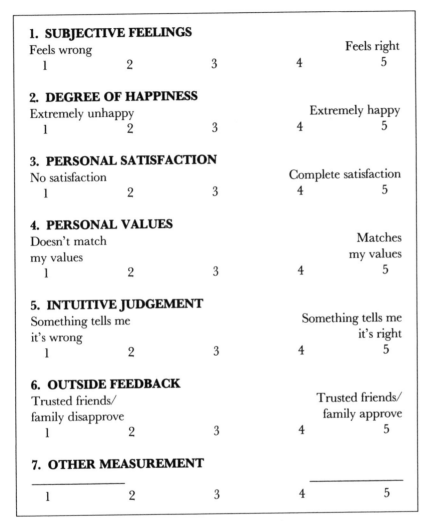

1. SUBJECTIVE FEELINGS
Feels wrong   Feels right
   1   2   3   4   5

2. DEGREE OF HAPPINESS
Extremely unhappy   Extremely happy
   1   2   3   4   5

3. PERSONAL SATISFACTION
No satisfaction   Complete satisfaction
   1   2   3   4   5

4. PERSONAL VALUES
Doesn't match   Matches
my values   my values
   1   2   3   4   5

5. INTUITIVE JUDGEMENT
Something tells me   Something tells me
it's wrong   it's right
   1   2   3   4   5

6. OUTSIDE FEEDBACK
Trusted friends/   Trusted friends/
family disapprove   family approve
   1   2   3   4   5

7. OTHER MEASUREMENT
_____   _____
   1   2   3   4   5

What makes us compromise (cheat)?

Sometimes we rely on others to determine our level of performance. Sometimes we are lazy and relax on standards we usually follow carefully. For example, you may lose contact with close friends, stop exercising, break a diet you are committed to or start missing appointments for no good reason.

What makes you lower your standards sometimes?

Do you notice that the following factors influence whether you meet your standards?

Approval: Do you let the approval of others influence your standards?

Fear: Are you afraid of failure or even success in reaching goals?

Convenience: Is it more convenient to change the standard or the level of performance ?

Time: Do you run out of time to do a good job or to even get started?

Overwhelming obstacles: Are the barriers so high that you think your standard can never be reached?

Cost: When it comes to real costs, does the sacrifice seem too great?

Fatigue: Are you tired from work, play, stress or handling too many details?

Which ones give you the most trouble? You can improve your personal standards of quality if you're aware of what stops you. Circle the number that indicates the degree to which each of the compromise factors affects your personal quality performance.

Approval of others
Major Barrier   No Problem
  1   2   3   4   5

Fear
Major Barrier   No Problem
  1   2   3   4   5

Convenience
Major Barrier   No Problem
  1   2   3   4   5

Time
Major Barrier   No Problem
  1   2   3   4   5

Overwhelming obstacles
Major Barrier   No Problem
  1   2   3   4   5

Cost

Major Barrier   No Problem

1   2   3   4   5

Fatigue

Major Barrier   No Problem

1   2   3   4   5

CHAPTER 3

THE THREE Cs OF QUALITY

'It is always with the best intentions that the worst work is done.'
Oscar Wilde

The intangible basics of quality: commitment, competence and communication.

The three Cs of quality – *Commitment*, *Competence* and *Communication* – are the intangible basics of your personal and organisational quality goals. You can't really touch or measure them, but no quality plan can succeed without them.

Commitment is the determined spirit of an Olympic swimmer who practises alone during hundreds of pre-dawn hours. *Competence* is the inner knowing of a well-trained pilot who uses all available knowledge – training, instruments and intuition – to make quick decisions. *Communication* is the critical personal contact and mutual agreement among managers and employees that makes work flow smoothly.

As a house is built on a concrete substructure, a quality plan is built on a foundation of commitment, competence and communication.

Cornerstone of quality

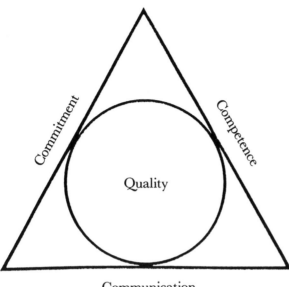

Commitment

A Harvard undergraduate, who knew himself well, left this note on his door for his roommate: 'Call me at seven. I absolutely have to get up at seven. Don't give up. Keep knocking until I answer.' At the bottom he wrote: 'Try again at nine.'

For a business to succeed, every employee must be committed to quality.

Commitment is a matter of degree. It is situational, as illustrated in the story above. Complete commitment to quality at work is defined as *a decisive personal or organisational choice to follow through an agreed plan of action.* Workers will be committed to qualify to the extent that management is committed.

Everyone is committed to something to some degree. Our commitments vary according to their importance and our ability to meet them. For a business to succeed in its commitment to quality, every employee must be committed to quality in every detail.

Example

Frank works as a keypunch operator typing coding sheets. He has been told, 'Don't think, just type what you see.' Frank knows he is typing obvious errors, such as 5 instead of a T. The programmer who receives the coding sheeets corrects the errors and sends them back to Frank for retyping, a time-consuming process.

One day Frank asked the programmer if he would stop by his desk to look at three obvious errors and amend them so he could type them correctly the first time, thus saving correction time later. While the programmer was still at his desk, Frank asked if he saw any other obvious errors that could be corrected now.

Does Frank have a
commitment to quality?　　Yes ☐　No ☐

To what degree would
you say he is committed?　High ☐　Average ☐　Low ☐

Rate your commitment

Degrees of commitment vary.

What is your level of commitment to quality in your organisation? Individuals make a difference, and many individuals working as a committed whole can revolutionise the quality and productivity of your organisation.

Listed below are personal and business situations that require a degree of commitment. Below them are four levels of commitment. Next to each situation put the appropriate number indicating which level of commitment you have to that item. Your answers are not right or wrong; they simply help you to know yourself and where your commitment lies. Knowing yourself is the first step in making changes.

Levels of commitment

1. Unwavering　　　　3. Casual

2. Diligent　　　　　4. When I'm in the mood

Personal and business situations

___ Marriage　___ Learning　　　　　　　　___ Helping others

___ Customers　___ Personal quality standards　___ Enjoying life

___ Family　　___ Organisational goals　　　___ Doing my best work

---

Competence

Along with commitment, quality goals require actions and attitudes based on competence. Competence can be described as know-how. Astronauts must be competent. The same is true of pharmacists, surgeons, firefighters and payroll personnel. Each must possess certain specific measurable skills, sound education, good intuitive judgement, an ability to apply related knowledge to solve problems and a responsible attitude. Competent people and quality work go hand in hand, because competent people make sure that they meet agreed requirements successfully.

People who do not perform their jobs competently are generally functioning at a low level in other areas of their lives as well. Without competence, employees are just surviving, rather than building quality into a product or service. On the other hand, successful quality programmes raise morale and improve competence through education, teamwork and incentive programmes.

When organisations implement quality improvements in an orderly way, they are exhibiting competence at the organisational level. They provide a master quality plan and involve all employees in its implementation. They also provide education about quality at all levels from top management down. The quality plan and the training are designed to improve competence. Improved competence will, in turn, improve quality. It also improves autonomy, teamwork, job security and profits. Organisations help people to develop competence by giving them the right tools and making them responsible for their work.

Lack of competence implies poor quality. It can be remedied by education and training.

Rate your competence

Listed below are areas of personal and professional competence. Under each topic, list those areas in which you would like to improve and those with which you are satisfied. With the help of your manager, family or friends, begin setting new competence goals for the areas you want to improve, and pat yourself on the back for the ones you are doing well.

Needs improvement	**I'm satisfied**
Job skills	
_____	_____
_____	_____

Education

_____   _____

_____   _____

Job experience

_____   _____

_____   _____

Communication skills

_____   _____

_____   _____

Solving problems

_____   _____

_____   _____

Making decisions

_____   _____

_____   _____

Leisure time

_____   _____

_____   _____

Organising

_____   _____

_____   _____

Others

_____   _____

_____   _____

Communication

George Bernard Shaw once said, 'The problem with communication is
the illusion that it is complete.' Communication problems are the

number one headache in most groups – families, companies or among friends. In spite of good intentions, people often have problems getting the message across to others effectively. Between the *sender* and *receiver* something gets lost in the translation. The weak links in communication include an *unclear purpose, garbled messges, barriers* (such as a hidden agenda, cultural differences, jargon, etc) and little or no *feedback*. The diagram below shows how quality communication works.

Communication is two-way between sender and receiver.

The purpose of communication* is to achieve mutual understanding. The definition of communication comes from the Latin word *communis*, meaning 'commonness', a *commonness of understanding*. A common understanding and mutual agreement cannot take place with one-way messages. Too often we send a message and assume it is received and understood the way we intended.

An American tourist in a Madrid restaurant wanted to order steak and mushrooms. He spoke no Spanish; the waiter knew no English. The diner drew a picture of a mushroom and a cow. The waiter left the table and returned a few moments later with an umbrella and a ticket for the bullfight.

Quality communication infinity model

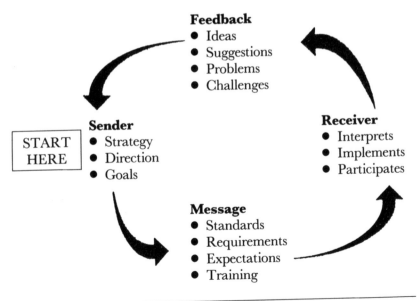

Feedback
- Ideas
- Suggestions
- Problems
- Challenges

Sender
- Strategy
- Direction
- Goals

START HERE

Receiver
- Interprets
- Implements
- Participates

Message
- Standards
- Requirements
- Expectations
- Training

* See *How to Communicate Effectively* by Bert Decker (Kogan Page).

In the model, both sides are responsible for success. For effective communication, the process is continuous until mutual understanding has been reached on the topic under discussion.

Guidelines for improved communication.

You can dramatically improve communication at home and at work if you and other key people remember these guidelines:

1. Determine the true *purpose* of your message.
2. Consider the *perception* of your audience.
3. Use the appropriate *channel* for delivery.
4. Obtain *feedback* to check mutual understanding.
5. Continually *improve* your communication skills.
6.. Take advantage of *training* opportunities.
7. *Reinforce* and *reward* good communication.

All groups have established communication systems, both formal and informal. For a quality programme to work effectively, an organisation must have a specific communication channel to send and receive information about the quality process.

Rate your communication
Quality is largely determined by how effectively you communicate in your personal and working life. We communicate more effectively when we understand the expectations in communication and set usable standards for ourselves.

Answer the questions below to clarify your communication expectations and to set your communication standards.

1. When you are the sender of information, what do you need from the receiver in order to know you were understood accurately?

   _____

   _____

2. What can you do to get what you need?

   _____

   _____

3. How can you meet other people's expectations in a communication situation?

_____

_____

4. What is a reasonable standard (or goal) to set for increasing the quality and effectiveness of your present communication?

_____

_____

5. How will you measure your standard?

_____

_____

6. What are some methods of improving communication about the quality programme in your organisation?

_____

_____

When you have finished, read the author's suggestions below.

Authors' comments

1. Feedback! Feedback! Feedback! Most of us do not *give* or *get* enough feedback to complete the communication loop. Feedback is written, verbal and non-verbal.
2. You can ask, 'What is your reaction to my suggestion (or statement)?' Also, look carefully for non-verbal signals, as they tell you more than words. When writing, ask for a written response.
3. Ask them how you can help them. Listen attentively. Provide verbal and non-verbal feedback. Paraphrase. Be open-minded.
4. Same as No 3, and *know your purpose.*
5. Self-evaluation and feedback from others. Do I feel more competent as a communicator? Are my projects completed in less time with fewer errors and less stress? Are people giving me better quality information in appropriate detail?

Spread the word about quality.

6. Communication (and plenty of it) is the best way to create quality awareness. Write the word 'QUALITY' on the walls and door mats, and write about it often in your organisation's newsletter. Create slogans – have a contest – and put quality statistics and improvement charts in the dining and recreation areas. Spread the word and say it with pride. Make quality an integral part of your company culture. Management should talk about quality regularly. Make it the first agenda item at department meetings.

Suggestions for communicating quality

- Start a newsletter about quality
- Make a video about quality
- Create quality groups
- Management – hold employee talk sessions
- Have suggestion boxes and forums
- Conduct status meetings
- Organise recognition parties for quality performance
- Write up policy statements (written and spoken)
- Talk to customers.

In his book *Quality Without Tears*, Philip Crosby tells the following story to illustrate an active approach to communicating a quality problem:

A management team was concerned about the errors in computer programming. The team members felt that these put an unusually heavy burden on the mainframe computer, since it was being used primarily for troubleshooting. They estimated a cost of £250,000 due to the software not being close enough to specification before troubleshooting began. Rather than just telling people about this, they borrowed ten brand-new BMWs and lined them all up in the front car park. Then they invited everybody out to 'see what troubleshooting costs us'. That made a big impression.

CHAPTER 4

YOUR ORGANISATION'S GOALS

'If you don't know where you're going, you will probably end up somewhere else.'

Laurence J Peters

Quality standards are based on an organisation's policies and goals. Goals create unity and group identity. Employees cannot help the organisation to reach its goals if they don't know what they are.*

An organisation's goals are usually divided into four categories:

An organisation's quality standards are based on policies and goals. Employees must know what these policies and goals are.

- The corporate mission statement
- Divisional objectives
- Each department's responsibilities
- Each employee's personal work responsibilities.

Goals are based on what the company wants to accomplish: solving problems, manufacturing products or providing services. For goals to succeed, everyone must understand them and agree to them. The corporate mission must be in agreement with divisional, departmental and individual work responsibilities.

Example

XYZ Ltd manufactures warblets. The manufacturing division of XYZ is very efficient and has set a production goal of 10,000 friblets

---

* For an excellent companion book get *How to Motivate People* by Twyla Dell (Kogan Page).

in the first quarter. One friblet is attached to each warblet. The corporate forecast calls for production of 5000 warblets. Is the manufacturing division working effectively towards organisational goals? How could they be more efficient in working with other departments or divisions to meet the organisation's goals?

There's a high cost in failing to communicate and agree on goals because, in their absence, everyone makes their own rules. In a service organisation, communication breakdowns such as these may account for as much as 30–40 per cent of operating costs.

Your mission role

Has your company issued a mission statement?

Can you answer the following questions about your organisation and your role in it? Knowing the part you play in the functioning of your organisation is an important step towards creating meaningful quality guidelines.

1. Describe your organisation's mission.

2. What is your personal role in helping to fulfil this mission?

3. List your division's or department's responsibilities as they relate to the organisation's mission.

4. Write down your personal work responsibilities.

5. List the responsibilities of your employees (if applicable).

Check your goal control

How does your organisation rate in 'goal control?' Tick the following to see how well you think your organisation's or department's goals are understood by its employees.

Yes	No	
☐	☐	Are your organisation's goals in writing?
☐	☐	Are they written in clear, simple language?
☐	☐	Are they widely distributed and available to everyone?
☐	☐	Are they consistent with other areas in the organisation?
☐	☐	Are they realistic?
☐	☐	Are they applicable to everyone?
☐	☐	Do they reflect management's respect for employees?
☐	☐	Are the people who set the goals talking about them and supporting them by example?
☐	☐	Do employees agree with the goals?
☐	☐	Is education available to support the goals?
☐	☐	Does management follow up when goals are set?
☐	☐	Do the goals set clear-cut deadlines?
☐	☐	Do they prescribe upper and lower limits if applicable?
☐	☐	Are they expressed in detail, including figures?

Setting quality standards

Goals are the single most important factor in controlling quality. The more specific they are, the better results you can expect. From goals come controls. Controls are another way of saying 'quality standards'. When you have an agreed standard of measurement, you can depend on the result.

Goals are the most important factor in establishing quality control.

Controls are methods of checking to see whether you are doing *what* you say you are going to do *when* you say you are going to do it. They help you to determine whether a product is fit for use. The bottom line is that goals and controls must be designed to make sure you meet your customer's needs.

The following steps are usually followed to establish controls or quality standards. These steps do not have to be complicated. In fact, they should be simple so that you will be able to implement them effectively. Tick the steps you follow regularly in your company.

47

Goal-setting checklist

Yes   No

☐   ☐   1. We have determined our corporate, divisional, departmental and personal goals.

☐   ☐   2. They are in agreement.

☐   ☐   3. We have decided what methods we will use for reaching our goals.

☐   ☐   4. We have set guidelines for acceptable work and our guidelines are standardised across the board.

☐   ☐   5. We are educating and training employees. We know our plan won't work if employees aren't informed and trained.

☐   ☐   6. We implement our work using our standard as guidelines. Our standards are incorporated into our organisation's technology.

☐   ☐   7. We check the results of the work *during* the process.

☐   ☐   8. We take immediate action to correct any problem or errors.

What's wrong with this story?

XYZ Manufacturing Group held a high-level organisational meeting at an exclusive country club. Organisation goals were reviewed and redefined. Each divisional manager established efficient new quality standards for employees and tight controls for enforcing the standards.

A quality control expert brought in by the XYZ chairman presented the most up-to-date methods of quality control, including sophisticated formulas to plan and chart results. The new procedures were finalised and adopted. Divisional managers received mandates to present them to their employees for immediate implementation. Employees were expected to adopt the new controls quickly and completely, and would be trained in the new procedures in the next six months.

In your opinion, what is wrong with this story? (See upside down box on page 49 for explanation.)

Answer. If you said that the plan lacked employee input, you are correct. The secret of success in any quality programme is that the people who set the standards must be the people who will be using them! True, upper-level managers will use them, but in this story they have set standards that will apply to all levels.

Most upper-level managers and engineering specialists do not know the nuts and bolts of the workplace. At one time they were involved in day-to-day production, but processes and conditions change rapidly and it is easy to lose touch with the daily reality of meeting customer requirements. Their expertise is the big picture.

Only by involving all employees in setting the standards can a company's quality programme be assured of success. If managers ignore employee input, they will be overlooking their most valuable assets for deciding what goals to adopt and the standards to measure them. When employees help to set standards, executives are assured that the people implementing them are committed to them.

The story retold

XYZ Manufacturing Group held an important yearly conference for all its managers and supervisors at an exclusive country club. The executive committee presented a proposed agenda of revised goals and projections for the coming year, including the implementation of a tight new quality control programme. Small groups discussed the goals and approved them or suggested additional revisions. Through evaluation and feedback, new and revised goals emerged with group consensus.

A quality control expert brought in by the chairman presented the most up-to-date methods of quality control. She then conducted small group sessions to help each department to adapt the procedures to its job responsibilities. The quality expert helped managers to outline a procedure for presenting the plan to their employees. The plan included asking for employee input and acceptance. She also helped the managers to design training programmes so that their employees would be able to implement the plan.

Divisional managers planned to meet again in six weeks to hear reports from their departmental managers. Based on these reports, they would then adjust their goals to reflect employee input. Final goals for the coming year were presented by the chairman at an all-company party in the following six weeks. Written confirmation was in everyone's mail within three days of the party.

Employees need to contribute to planned quality procedures.

49

◄ CHAPTER 5 ►

PS: THE PERFECTION STANDARD

'If you believe in unlimited quality, and act in all your business dealings with total integrity, the rest will take care of itself.'

Frank Perdue

PS = Perfection Standard or Personal Satisfaction.

PS is the **Perfection Standard** that you apply to your work to achieve quality. You can also use PS to refer to Personal Satisfaction, because that should be the result of working to agreed specifications.

What *is* the 'perfect' report, the 'perfect' sales call, the 'perfect' widget? Quality control experts hold varying opinions about what standard should be used to determine when finished work is 'perfect' enough to release to the next process or to the customer. Quality control experts use such terms as *zero defects* and *error-free*, which mean that a product or service contains no errors. That is one standard.

The goal of PS with zero defects.

Some quality experts believe that errors are inescapable because humans are not perfect. The **Perfection Standard** suggests that people and organisations should decide how closely they will approximate perfection in their products or services, based on their customers' needs. This **Perfection Standard** should be zero defects if possible. However, PS takes into account that peaches for display in a gourmet supermarket are of a higher quality than those selected in a food processing plant for pie filling.

Perfection should be thought of as a goal rather than as something that can literally be achieved. A **Perfection Standard** then is a no-nonsense written guideline to help employees to perfect their services or products according to specific agreed requirements. The result is a

50

proud employee, a suitable product or service, and a satisfied customer. PS helps to avoid the 'get-by blues'.

PS (Perfection Standards)

Perfection Standards make everyone's job easier. They allow people to depend on each other. When you have a PS, you have a goal to work towards. As the Cheshire Cat said to Alice, 'If you don't know where you wish to go, then any road will do.' With PS, we know which road we want and we have signposts to help us get there.

Characteristics of Perfection Standards.

The following are 20 characteristics of useful Perfection Standards:

1. Your Perfection Standards should come as close to zero defects as is humanly possible for your product or service.
2. They should be planned and agreed by all affected employees, including customers when possible.
3. They should be stated, clearly and completely, in writing.
4. They must satisfy your customers' requirements.
5. They must be workable and understandable.
6. No one must deviate from the standards for any reason once they are established.
7. They must be supported by upper management (or they won't work).
8. A PS evolves. If the PS is not working or becomes outdated, it should be changed.
9. New Perfection Standards should be added as needed. All affected employees must agree to the new PS.
10. They should be written in a way that identifies for customers exactly what they can expect to receive.
11. They should reflect a 'perfection' attitude.
12. They must be results orientated.
13. They should include recognition for performance.
14. They must be taken seriously.
15. They must be included in an ongoing educational programme.
16. They must reflect organisational goals.
17. They must be set for *all* functions of a department or a division.
18. They should not be dependent on inspection. They should be followed regardless of inspection. They should be inspected when something goes wrong, and the root cause should be found and corrected.
19. They should be created and met with care.
20. They must be communicated effectively and continually.

Putting PS to work: 'Just do it!'

Measure your performance.

In order to set Perfection Standards, you need a way to measure your performance. The Seven-Step Plan that follows will help you to set and measure your PS. With proper motivation, Perfection Standards are easy to establish. This plan contains no magic; all you have to do is follow it step by step. It's a foolproof way to improve the quality of your work immediately.

Part of the PS Seven-Step Plan is to define your work by what you *contribute* rather than by what you *do*. In other words, how do *you* make the company better?

Example

Mary is a training consultant in technical education. When she evaluated what she did in her job, she said at first that she provided technical training programmes for employees. After a discussion with her manager, Mary broadened her definition to state that she helped to develop competent people. Stating what she contributes is a positive way of stating what she does.

The Seven-Step Plan: a preview

List your work responsibilities and establish goals for improving quality in seven steps.

The Seven-Step Plan outlined below helps you to identify your most important work responsibilities and establish specific goals for improving the quality of each task, as necessary. These steps provide a clear, consistent blueprint of your work priorities and will help you to get things done.

Step 1. List your most important tasks.
Step 2. Rank your tasks by categories.
Step 3. State the end result(s) of each task.
Step 4. List activities that achieve the end result.
Step 5. Select your measurement standards.
Step 6. Select a P-A-S Option for each task.*
Step 7. List specific goals to support your P-A-S Options.

Bonus. You can also use the Seven-Step Plan to teach other employees to set quality goals.

---

* See page 31 if you need a reminder.

Cornerstone of quality 2

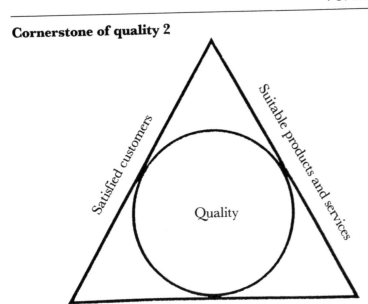

The Seven-Step Plan for measuring quality performance

Step 1. List your most important tasks

Based on your organisation's goals and your own job description, select the three most important tasks you perform at work and rank them in order of importance. Later you can expand your list to include other tasks you want to measure. By beginning with the three most important, you avoid 'paralysis by analysis'.

Most important tasks.

Task 1. _____

Task 2. _____

Task 3. _____

Step 2. Rank your tasks by categories

Rank each task on a 1–5 scale (with 5 being the highest) for the following categories:

Categories of task.

	Task 1	Task 2	Task 3
(a) Helps to meet organisation goals	____	____	____

(b) Helps to meet departmental goals _____ _____ _____

(c) Meets my job description _____ _____ _____

(d) Provides personal satisfaction _____ _____ _____

(e) Contributes to the organisation _____ _____ _____

(f) Makes work smoother for colleagues _____ _____ _____

(g) Creates profit for the organisation _____ _____ _____

(h) Helps to put the organisation in a leading position _____ _____ _____

(i) Provides long-term value _____ _____ _____

Step 3. State the end results(s) of each task

Results of tasks.

Write down the end result of each of the three priority tasks you listed in Step 1. What does each task look like when it is complete? These completed tasks are your product or service that will meet your final expectation or the expectations of your manager or customer.

Example:

Task: *Write service orders*   End result: *Service order delivered to maintenance*

Task 1. _____   End result: _____

Task 2. _____   End result: _____

Task 3. _____   End result: _____

Step 4. List activities that achieve the end result

Achieving the results.

What specific activities do you perform to achieve the end results listed above?

54

Example:

Task: *Write service orders* End result: *Deliver orders to maintenance*

Tasks performed: *Take information from customer.*
Fill in the form

Task 1. ――――――― End result: ―――――――――

――――――― Tasks performed: ―――――――

―――――――――

Task 2. ――――――― End result: ―――――――――

――――――― Tasks performed: ―――――――

―――――――――

Task 3. ――――――― End result: ―――――――――

――――――― Tasks performed: ―――――――

―――――――――

Step 5. Select your measurement standards

From the list below decide which standards you will use to measure the three tasks. Your measurement helps you to determine whether your work is satisfactory or needs improvement. Not every function of every task needs measurement.

Measurement standards.

Task 1 I will measure:	**Task 2** I will measure:	**Task 3** I will measure:
☐ Quantity	☐ Q	☐ Q
☐ Quality	☐ Ql	☐ Ql
☐ Cost	☐ C	☐ C
☐ Time	☐ T	☐ T
☐ Accuracy	☐ A	☐ A
☐ Customer satisfaction	☐ Cs	☐ Cs
☐ Flexibility	☐ F	☐ F

Step 6. Select a P-A-S Option for each task

Appropriate option for each task.

Select your P-A-S Option below. Your P-A-S Option is the standard that is the most appropriate choice for each activity. Which option is best for your specific tasks?

> **PERFECTION Option:** No mistakes, no defects, inflexible
>
> **AVERAGE Option:** Past results are fine, very flexible
>
> **STRETCH Option:** Reasonable difficulty, little flexibility

For many tasks, average is appropriate. Your challenge will be to maintain your P-A-S Option choice. Remember, choose your options carefully and then perform them as agreed.

Step 7. List specific goals to support your P-A-S Options

In Task 1, what is your most important measurement (Step 5)? _____

Your P-A-S Option choice (Step 6) for Task 1: _____

List three specific goals that will help you to maintain your P-A-S Option choice:

1. _____

2. _____

3. _____

In Task 2, what is your most important measurement (Step 5)? _____

Your P-A-S Option choice (Step 6) for Task 2: _____

List three specific goals that will help you to maintain your P-A-S Option choice:

1. _____

2. _____

3. _____

In Task 3, what is your most important measurement (Step 5)? _____

Your P-A-S Option choice (Step 6) for Task 3: _____

List three specific goals that will help you to maintain your P-A-S Option choice:

1. —————————————————————————————

2. —————————————————————————————

3. —————————————————————————————

The goals you have set in Step 7 are your initial steps for measuring and improving the quality of the most important tasks you perform. Each month you can add a new task, evaluate the steps and set an improvement goal. At the same time you can re-evaluate your original goals and decide whether you want to make changes.

An action-orientated quality plan

Quality challenges will not disappear when you initiate your Seven-Step Plan, but you will have an organised method of coping with those problems. The sort of challenges that turn up are problems to be solved, opportunities or new goals to be met. The chart below suggests another easy method for defining challenges as they occur in your work environment.

Use the Seven-Step Plan to deal with quality challenges.

Challenges	Core tasks	Completion date	Who is responsible
There are no quality guide-lines for sales force.	Do Seven-Step Plan quality exercises to set three priorities for sales force.	15 October	Tom Clifton Gloria Lucas
PS plan for data processing typing pool is outdated.	Choose new P-A-S Options.	30 September	Doris Bell Louise Hanson

Getting results

Once you have adopted your Perfection Standards you must show results. When you examine the results of applying your PS, ask yourself the following questions:

Did you receive the results you expected?
Did you receive any benefits you didn't expect? What are they?
How can your positive results be made even better?
Would you make changes based on the results? What kind?
Are there any negative results? What are they?
Can you change them? How?

◀ CHAPTER 6 ▶

THE 'HOW-TO' OF QUALITY

'There will be two kinds of companies in the future – companies which have implemented total quality, and companies which are out of business.'

Robert Millar

This chapter addresses basic quality issues from a 'how-to' point of view. In his book, *Believe and Achieve*, Sam Cypert tells this story about the legendary coach of the Green Bay Packers football team, Vince Lombardi and the basics.

Once, after the Green Bay Packers football team had played a particularly bad game, Coach Lombardi got on the bus, held up the ball, and said, 'Gentlemen, this is a football.' From the back of the bus, a player spoke up and said, 'Coach, slow down; you're going too fast for us ...'

Because quality is not an object like a football, it is harder to identify. However, we *can* identify individual components of quality. In this chapter we will introduce nine action-orientated components of a quality programme, and give you some basic guidelines for addressing each. You will be given exercises to help you to apply these principles in your own work.

Identify the individual components of a quality programme.

These are the ten 'how-to' components of a quality programme. They are:

1. Identify and solve quality problems
2. Ensure customer satisfaction
3. Measure results
4. Reward quality performance
5. Set up quality groups
6. Provide quality training
7. Assess the cost of quality
8. Establish your quality programme
9. Support your quality programme
10. Make quality work.

1. How to identify and solve quality problems

Problems must be prevented to achieve quality.

Quality is based on problem prevention. We can prevent a problem only when we understand the process. Perfection Standard (PS) is the means for preventing problems. Even if your goal is zero defects, problems will occur from time to time because the people, environment and materials change over time. *A commitment to quality means stopping the process and dealing with the problem.* The following steps will help you to identify and solve quality problems.

Find the problem. Problems do not usually appear without some warning. Managers committed to PS check with their people often and in person to see how things are going. Managers and supervisors should visit each part of the workplace with a purpose in mind. In his book *A Passion for Excellence*, Tom Peters calls this Management By Wandering Around (MBWA).

While wandering around, managers compare what they see to the PS. They enquire about potential problems and create a supportive environment in which employees feel free to report problems. (If management has not clearly defined goals and PS, however, workers may feel uncomfortable and be unwilling to discuss problems.) Management controls problem situations by knowing where the opportunities are for errors and by acting quickly when they occur. They involve everyone in working together to solve the problem.

Identify problems by their effects. Production is slowed by 20 per cent (effect) because of a flu epidemic (problem). A customer is angry (effect) because he had to hold on for three minutes (problem). Effects indicate that something is happening in the process that does not meet PS.

Check through the effects to the cause. Causes are the reasons for the problems. Some reasons may be obvious. Other root causes are less obvious. Like the skin of an onion, each layer is a suspected cause and you must peel away the layers to find the *root cause*. Unless root causes are found and dealt with, the problem will probably recur.

When you have identified the root cause, communicate the problem to everyone involved and refer to your written PS. If the PS is outdated or does not address the problem, it should be changed.

Effect: 20 per cent decrease in productivity
Cause: Flu epidemic
Root cause: Flu vaccination programme not offered to company employees

Effect: Angry customer
Cause: Held on for three minutes
Root cause: Overloaded phone lines

Correct the root cause. Involve everyone in finding the root cause and correcting it. Possible corrections to the problems just defined are: (1) Vaccinate all consenting employees immediately and set up a contingency plan for the next flu season. (2) Add additional telephone lines and provide extra personnel to answer phones during peak hours.

Reinforce PS to ensure prevention in the future. Prevention results in quality, correction after the fact does not. Although it's difficult to prove, experts suggest a 10 to 1 payback with the preventive approach. It is not a flashy, award-filled approach that singles out heroes for successfully putting out fires. Rather it is a low-key strategy like preventive medicine, which simply maintains organisational health and quality without fanfare. The result is that costs are reduced and the mission is accomplished.

Recheck to make sure the problem has not recurred. Many problems do not disappear completely with the first solution, and it is important to check periodically to make sure quality remains in place.

Problem-solving checklist

Here is a checklist to help you to pinpoint personal attitudes and work situations that can create problems if they are not approached with a positive attitude. Tick those that apply to you and evaluate your score at the bottom of the checklist.

Yes No

1. ☐ ☐ I work actively to support management decisions regarding quality in our organisation.

2. ☐ ☐ I keep my ego in check and work as a team member to complete quality goals.

3. ☐ ☐ I am satisfied with quality as it is and wonder what all the fuss over quality is about.

4. ☐ ☐ I rely on my own experience and seldom seek the opinions of others when completing quality goals.

5. ☐ ☐ I am mindful of tunnel vision and always try to see the good of the whole organisation in my quality goals.

6. ☐ ☐ I work enthusiastically towards my quality goals in order to keep morale high in my department.

7. ☐ ☐ I refrain from living in the past when things were simpler, and deal realistically with the more complex workplace of today.

8. ☐ ☐ I seldom take advantage of the professional training in quality performance and problem solving offered by my organisation.

Answers. Yes: 1,2,5,6,7. No: 3,4,8. If you have these answers, you are on the quality bandwagon and are part of the solution rather than part of the problem. If you have other answers than these, check your attitude towards quality and adjust accordingly.

Problem-solving exercise

1. Choose a product or service in your department that has a recurring problem. State the problem. (Problems are deviations from standards.)

2. List the effects or consequences of the problem. (All problems reveal themselves by their effects.)

3. List the *root causes*. Be objective. Pointing the finger of blame at a person creates a smoke screen that keeps you from finding the real cause. Consult the people involved if you are uncertain about causes.

4. Decide what preventive action you can take.

5. Follow up to verify your results.

FACE the Facts

You can summarise the previous problem-solving exercise by remembering this mnemonic. It will help you to *FACE the facts* and become a world-class problem solver.

Find the facts
Analyse alternatives
Choose and implement
Evaluate the results

---

2. How to ensure customer satisfaction

'Quality is what the customer says it is.'
Dr Armand Feigenbaum

The first and truest test of quality is whether a product or service meets your customers' requirements. The pay-off for PS comes from a customer's trust that a product or service has been reliable over a long period. Your company is assured of success when all your products or services succeed and your customers recommend you by saying, 'We have confidence in everything they sell.'

Customers want a reliable product or service to meet their requirements.

Most customers are easy to please. They simply want us to do what we say we are going to do when we say we are going to do it. They are also pleased, and surprised, when we take time to follow up and ask if they are satisfied. The idea of phoning is easy but its implementation is rare. Imagine how many compliments and good ideas you would receive if you viewed follow-up calls as opportunities rather than threats.

Some interesting statistics tell why companies lose customers:

1%	of lost customers die.
3%	move away.
4%	just naturally float.
5%	change on a friend's recommendations.
9%	can buy it cheaper somewhere else.
10%	are chronic complainers.
68%	go elsewhere because the people they deal with are indifferent to their needs.

Our customers are not the frosting on the cake – they *are* the cake. The frosting is an improved reputation and higher profits as a result of a quality job.*

Encourage customers to complain

You and your customers should be friends. Apart from skilled workers, the best improvement ideas come from customers. A wise organisation uses the information to improve quality and service. Several Japanese companies have been encouraging consumer feedback by including this statement in their product packaging:

'Accepting bad products without complaint is not necessarily a virtue.'

Most customers don't complain. They quietly switch to another product or service. However, they would probably remain loyal if they were encouraged to complain and something was done to improve the product or service as a result.

Encourage feedback from customers.

You can encourage your customers to help you to make a better product by asking them to complain. The following guidelines are helpful:

1. Make it easy for customers to complain. Use complaint forms and 0800 (free) phone numbers and check on customers personally for their feedback.
2. Listen to the complaint. Ask questions. Ask for suggestions.
3. Make sure the complaints reach the right people.
4. Act quickly and with goodwill to solve the problem.
5. Replace defective products immediately, without charge.
6. Take positive steps to prevent the problem's recurrence.

---

* For an excellent companion book on customer satisfaction read *Customer Service* by Malcolm Peel (Kogan Page).

To bring the concept of quality closer to home, you can apply the same tests to your *internal* customers as to your external customers. Think of your internal customers as your personal customers, those colleagues who receive the work that you complete. Your personal customers should be treated even better than your outside customers, because *you'll be seeing them again*. The following worksheet will help you to identify your personal customers and your quality goals in relation to them.

Personal customer worksheet

1. My personal customers are:

2. My PS goal for my product or service is (Review Step 7 of your Seven-Step Plan) shown on page 56.

3. Answer yes or no to the following questions:

Yes No

☐ ☐ Do I establish my PS with my personal customers in mind?

☐ ☐ Do I talk to my personal customers regularly?

☐ ☐ Do I ask if I'm pleasing them?

☐ ☐ Do I ask my customers if they are satisfied?

☐ ☐ Do I request honest feedback or suggestions?

☐ ☐ Do I look at my product or service from a 'do unto others' point of view?

☐ ☐ Do I correct errors and handle problems quickly and completely?

☐ ☐ Do I recheck to make sure that problems do not recur?

☐ ☐ Do I use my product or service myself (where applicable)?

3. How to measure results

Kids count marbles, merchants count pounds and Casanovas count dates! Everything we do can be measured. In the work setting we need exact and accountable measurement systems that pinpoint performance while leaving room for intuitive measures as well. The personal standards evaluations in Chapter 2 are examples of intuitive, subjective evaluation.

Collect information to see where you stand.

The first step in measuring results is to collect information to see where you stand. This *baseline data* is used as a benchmark to see how effective future changes and efforts will be in improving performance. Poor data leads to poor decisions. Take the time to measure well and get the employee whose work is being measured to support the idea.

What to measure
- Quantity (pounds, number of units produced, pages)
- Cost (pounds, over budget, under budget, profit, loss, break even)
- Time (minutes, hours, overtime, 'undertime', time saved)
- Accuracy (mistakes, defects, proximity, inches, preciseness, corrections)
- Flexibility (speed in changing and adapting to new requirements)
- Customer satisfaction (compliments, complaints, increase in orders).

When to measure
The best time to measure is when you can get the most accurate picture of what is happening. This 'snapshot' should record reality without affecting the results. If the measurement affects the results, you are not recording performance, but the reaction to the measurement. Sometimes you want to do this – to use measurement as a motivator. The drawback is that it no longer records reality.

Tools for measuring
- Observation
- Customer surveys (see sample that follows)
- Before and after measures (pre and post tests)
- Primary data that you collect
- Secondary data that you get from others
- Line graphs (data points are charted over days/weeks/months and connected with a line)
- Bar graphs (cumulative data is stacked in bar form to show comparisons of total time, money, defects or hours worked)
- Control charts (line or bar graphs are used along with horizontal lines to show the upper and/or lower limits of acceptable performance).

Remember when you measure
- Inform people about the measurement system.

- Give the reasons for measuring.
- Let people know what will happen with the results.
- Measure in such a way that performance is not affected by the act of measuring.
- Measure unobtrusively without spying.

Customer quality survey

Example

We appreciate your business and want to continue providing high quality products and services that meet your specifications. We would also like to do it on time. Please answer the following questions to assist us in our efforts to meet high quality standards.

Customer questionnaire.

Rating scale: 1 = Lowest score, 5 = Highest score

1. How would you rate our responsiveness to your needs?   1   2   3   4   5

2. How would you rate the delivery of the product/service?   1   2   3   4   5

3. What is the rating for our speed in serving you?   1   2   3   4   5

4. Are we changing with your changing needs?   1   2   3   4   5

5. How would you rate our face-to-face interaction?   1   2   3   4   5

6. How would you rate our telephone interaction?   1   2   3   4   5

7. What's the rating for our follow-up (after the sale)?   1   2   3   4   5

8. What's your overall impression of our quality?   1   2   3   4   5

9. Do our personal standards support our working relationship?   1   2   3   4   5

10. How would you rate the quality of our communication?   1   2   3   4   5

General comments:

4. How to reward quality performance

Formal or informal, your reward system should recognise goal-related activities.

Don't you love getting things! It's nice to get gifts on birthdays and at Christmas. It's also pleasing to receive those little intangible gifts of appreciation, compliments or recognition. The reward system in your organisation may be very formal or quite casual. A reward can be a friendly letter or memo. What it should do is recognise and promote goal-related activities.

What to reward
- Reward results more than effort.
- Reward efforts that directly support specific goals.
- Reward critical performance rather than routine tasks.
- Reward performance that sets good examples for others.

When to reward
- As soon after the performance as possible.
- When the example would improve employee performance.
- When it will reinforce your quality commitment to your customers.
- When it reinforces organisational and personal standards.

How to reward
- Reward in public rather than in private.
- Start by rewarding frequently.
- Gradually require more/better performance before rewarding.
- Be sure to reward the little things that contribute to quality.
- Be specific about what is being rewarded.
- Be as sincere as possible.
- Show your feelings and appreciation for the performance.
- Tie the good performance to profitability and customer satisfaction.

5. How to set up quality groups

'In my opinion, the real strength of our Quality Enhancement Process is its absolute reliance on input from the people who know the problems – and how to solve them.'

John Ankeny

There are a number of structures used in quality-conscious companies to support their commitment to quality. The main ones are:

Quality circles

If you work in a large organisation you have probably heard of or participated in quality circles. These are groups of workers who meet voluntarily to learn how to improve quality and productivity and then apply these skills to organisational problems. The original idea revolved around weekly meetings that included:

- Leader and member training
- Project selection
- Data collection/verification
- Implementing solutions
- Management presentations
- New project selection.

The authors' experience while managing quality circles led to specific changes that gave the programme quick and visible results in order to maintain the support of the organisation. These included:

- Shorter projects
- Selecting only projects with a direct organisational impact
- 'Mini' management presentations for updating and reducing member anxiety.

These and other formalised changes have been tested by hundreds of groups over the past few years. A more recent development, the quality team, continues the evolution by requiring wider participation and results in a dramatic increase in the number of projects completed each year.

The quality council

A variation on the quality circle concept is the idea of a corporate quality council. The council is made up of members of each division of the organisation. It also includes members from each level of management, supervision and first-line employment. The group meets regularly to identify, analyse and correct quality issues within the firm. They perform interdepartmental problem-solving functions.

Rolestorming

Rolestorming is a combination of several group ideas using a technique developed by the authors to increase consensus building, creativity and

In large organisations workers meet in groups to learn how to improve quality and apply these skills to organisational problems.

- **quality circles**

- **quality council**

- **rolestorming**

quality performance. The composition of the group, meeting times and other details should be tailored to your organisation's needs.

Rolestorming is part of a process called Profile-Scans* which solicits, refines and focuses group input in about one hour. Rolestorming asks each participant to combine roleplaying and brainstorming to expand idea-generating power in the room. It goes like this:

1. Pretend you are someone who is a stakeholder but not present at the meeting.
2. Consider his or her ideas, goals, problems and concerns.
3. From his or her perspective, brainstorm ideas and comments about the quality issue being discussed.

The Q-panel

• **Q-panel**

A Q-panel is an educational forum featuring a group of internal and external authorities, lecturers and practitioners. In practice, it brings expert knowledge on quality issues and makes them personally available to individual employees. A variation on the Q-panel is a special meeting where individual experts or department heads are invited to speak in depth about their expertise in quality areas.

Case study.

Ann's story

Ann is in charge of the quality programme in her department. Her department is responsible for customer support for a large software development company. The department has set Perfection Standards of:

1. Answering customer calls by the third ring.
2. Treating all customers as they themselves would like to be treated.
3. Having a two-hour turnaround on all calls.

Although Ann is committed to quality, she is shy, and when she sees a problem she hesitates to interfere. Lately people in her department have gone back to their old ways of handling customer calls and the new quality goals seem to be forgotten. Which of the following should Ann do to get her department back on track?

_____ Call a quality meeting of the whole department.

_____ Ignore the problem.

* Profile-Scans is a trademark of MANFIT-Management Fitness Systems.

_____ Talk to her manager.

_____ Continue to set a quality example.

_____ Scold employees for not meeting quality goals.

_____ Attend an assertiveness course.

_____ Check with people individually to see how they are doing with their goals.

_____ Take a survey to see what the quality problems are.

_____ Set up a Q-panel and do some rolestorming.

_____ Leave the organisation.

Answers. Ann should talk to her manager first. She should explain her shyness and ask for help. With her manager's support she should check with people individually to see how they are coping with their goals. A survey would also be helpful. After collecting the feedback she should call a meeting of the department and set up a Q-panel as a means of solving some of the quality issues. In the meantime, Ann should continue to set a quality example, and perhaps sign up for a course to increase her confidence.

The authors' experience of consulting in finance, high technology and government organisations has shown why some quality groups succeed over a long period and others fail rather quickly. Here are some guidelines for creating successful groups.

Guidelines for quality groups.

Forming a group

When starting any type of quality group, be sure to lay the initial groundwork before proceeding. Include everyone by informing them about the purpose of the group, what its goals are, and what support it will need to be effective.

1. Start with volunteers who perform well.
2. Teach, train and educate them about personal and work quality.
3. Set goals and priorities with management.
4. Expand participation to include more of the workforce.

Running a group

1. Be/recruit an enthusiastic and quality-educated leader.

2. Gather input and ideas from the entire organisation.
3. Identify specific duties and results for each member.
4. Focus efforts on critical organisational priorities.
5. Continue to expand participation.

Participating in a group
1. Attend and participate as agreed.
2. Work with other group members and with others in the organisation.
3. Speak your mind when you agree or disagree.

Selecting projects
1. Get as much management input as you can.
2. Stick to critical organisational priorities.
3. Start with short-term projects to build confidence and skill.

Presenting to management
1. Schedule sessions when there is something important to present.
2. Arrange for the entire group to participate.
3. Get feedback on their satisfaction with the group's current activities.
4. Ask them about changes in plans, priorities and strategies.

When to disband a group
1. When organisational quality goals cease to be met.
2. When support for the group is absent.
3. As soon as you have solved all quality issues!

Quality group checklist
The following checklist will help you to plan a quality group. If you answer yes to each question you are ready to meet as a quality group and begin discussing quality problems and solutions. Three guidelines are helpful: (1) Be creative. (2) Be positive. (3) Have fun!

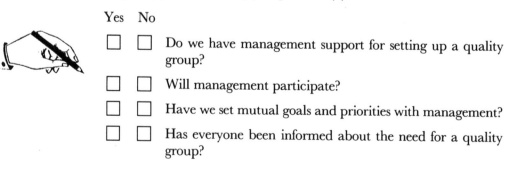

Yes No

☐ ☐ Do we have management support for setting up a quality group?

☐ ☐ Will management participate?

☐ ☐ Have we set mutual goals and priorities with management?

☐ ☐ Has everyone been informed about the need for a quality group?

☐ ☐ Do we have a meeting room?

☐ ☐ Have we sent memos to people inviting them to participate? (The group should be voluntary.)

☐ ☐ Do we have a designated leader who is experienced in running a quality group?

☐ ☐ Have we decided on a format for the group (quality circle, quality council, Q-panel, other)?

☐ ☐ Do we know specifically what quality issues we want to discuss?

☐ ☐ Do we have an agenda?

☐ ☐ Has someone been designated to record the results of the meeting and send written summaries to everyone concerned?

☐ ☐ Have we planned a specific time to begin and end?

☐ ☐ Have we included time for discussion and breaks?

☐ ☐ Have we selected a name for our group?

☐ ☐ Have we gathered input and ideas from everyone involved?

☐ ☐ Have we decided how we will get feedback from the group after the meeting?

6. How to provide quality training

'Quality begins and ends with education.'

Kaoru Ishikawa

'The first and most important component of management is training.'

Peter F Drucker

Thomas Gilbert reinforces training in his book *Human Competence* by stating:

Successful management equals
A. Clear expectations
B. Adequate guidance for performance
C. Best possible tools

73

D. Generous rewards

E. Useful training.

Success in training involves focusing on critical organisational needs and taking the long-term approach.

Training can focus on current skill needs or future development. Personal and work quality will project attitudes, skills, opinions and values that have been learned over time. The best training programmes recognise that old habits are hard to break. This means you'll get better success by focusing training on critical organisational needs and by taking the long-term approach. Training is a personal and a management function.

Tips on training

1. Tie it in with organisational objectives.
2. Get input from management and those being trained.
3. Check to see whether the specific objectives are being met.
4. Look for on-the-job applications of the training skills.
5. *Never* portray training as a luxury.
6. Never *start* cutting costs by cutting training.

Your start-up 'to do' list

(Tick those you plan to incorporate into your programme.)

Plan to do: By date:

———   ———   Completed needs assessment to develop objectives

———   ———   Budget (for complete programme)

———   ———   Advisers identified and updated

———   ———   Geographical location selected

———   ———   Types of instructor identified

———   ———   Instructors hired/trained

———   ———   Course objectives double-checked

———   ———   Materials written/prepared

———   ———   Specific room locations selected and reserved

———   ———   Equipment identified, ordered and tested

——	——	Method of evaluating results selected
——	——	Student selection process outlined
——	——	Students notified in advance (dates, locations, etc)
——	——	Process to make corrections or modifications outlined

Other ideas

——	——
——	——

Rate your quality training programme

Answer the following questions to rate your quality training programme.

1. We have an active quality training programme in our organisation.
   Yes ——— No ———

2. Our quality education programme is solidly supported by upper management.
   Yes ——— No ———

3. Management provides the following input for our quality education programme:

4. Our quality training programme can be described as follows:

5. Employees provide the following input for our quality training programme:

6. Our quality training programme has the following strengths:

7. We can improve our quality training programme in the following ways:

8. Follow-up on quality training in our organisation is achieved in the following ways:

9. On-the-job applications of quality training are implemented as follows:

10. Quality education is cost effective in our organisation.
Yes _____ No _____

7. How to assess the cost of quality

Cost is an important baseline for improvement in quality.

How much does quality cost? This is a problem – you need a way to evaluate the price you pay for quality now and the price you would pay if you put a new or more rigorous quality programme in place. After it is in place, you need to evaluate costs continually in order to monitor the programme. Cost is an important baseline for improvement. First of all, let's define the cost of quality.

The cost of quality is:
What it costs to prevent and correct problems.
The combined price of conformity and non-conformity.

Philip Crosby refines this definition further, and says that quality costs fall into three areas: *prevention* costs, *appraisal* costs and *failure* costs.

Conformity is ensuring that things are done right the first time. It includes identifying requirements and specifications, communicating requirements and specifications, and using a preventive approach to do things right the first time.

Non-conformity leads to redoing things and to unmet expectations. It wastes time and materials, creates the need for heavy inspection, and costs ten times more to correct than to prevent.

You should periodically evaluate the cost of quality, both in your business and in your personal life. When too little attention is paid to prevention, the cost of problems goes up; this is one way to alert yourself to a slackening of quality controls.

Quality in business. To assess the cost of quality at work, be sure to include the cost of:

- Activities for preventing problems occurring
- Inspecting products or services
- Breakdowns and defects that occur *before* delivering the product/service
- Breakdowns and defects that occur *after* delivering the product/service.

Personal quality. The personal costs of quality include the time, money and emotional energy used to learn and practise high-quality living. It also includes the lost time, goodwill, money and opportunity when we don't. Be sure to include the costs of:

- Preventive education or 'learn it before you need it'
- Preventive planning and strategising
- Time taken to develop standards
- Problems caused to ourselves by not meeting standards
- Problems caused to others by not meeting standards
- Problems caused by having the wrong PS standards or P-A-S Options.

Keep a cost diary

On a diary similar to the one shown on page 78, keep track of costs you incur as a result of not meeting your quality goals. These can be personal as well as professional costs and they can be time or people related (lost time, hurt feelings) as well as pounds and pence. Also keep track of your quality gains each month, especially as you add new goals to your Seven-Step Plan.

Cost Diary

January	**February**	**March**
Costs	Costs	Costs
personal *professional*	*personal* *professional*	*personal* *professional*
savings based on prevention	*savings based on prevention*	*savings based on prevention*
April	**May**	**June**
Costs	Costs	Costs
personal *professional*	*personal* *professional*	*personal* *professional*
savings based on prevention	*savings based on prevention*	*savings based on prevention*
July	**August**	**September**
Costs	Costs	Costs
personal *professional*	*personal* *professional*	*personal* *professional*
savings based on prevention	*savings based on prevention*	*savings based on prevention*
October	**November**	**December**
Costs	Costs	Costs
personal *professional*	*personal* *professional*	*personal* *professional*
savings based on prevention	*savings based on prevention*	*savings based on prevention*

8. How to establish your quality programme

You have probably seen various quality programmes in action during your career. Some have failed and some have succeeded. Here are some guidelines for establishing a programme that will succeed. Use them to start a new programme or adjust your current one.

Guidelines for establishing a successful quality programme.

Overall plan. Every quality consultant, book or workshop suggests that you start with a systematic plan that covers your goals and objectives for the programme. A few hours spent on planning save days and months of wasted time later.

Commitment and support. Identify the commitment and support that will be needed to keep your quality efforts supported, visible and rewarded when there is success. Design your programme before forming groups or identifying problems.

Education and training. Bite the bullet! Your programme will fail if you don't hammer out what your workforce know and what they need to know. The difference is what the education and training programmes must cover. A sporadic and superficial overview may build emotions and morale for a while, but it won't last. Line up resources at the college level, among private firms and individuals who can assist in the effort.

Tools and materials. Course materials are a good start. Supplement what you can offer employees by adding books, videotapes and audio-cassette packages. A mandatory system of checks, reviews and accountability for the subject content *will create better quality.*

Participation and involvement. People want to be involved. And believe it or not, they have great ideas that will work wonders. Ask them, train them and give them the proper tools. Follow up with quick implementation of their solid ideas to start a steady stream of productivity and quality improvement.

Measurement indicators. Select 6 to 10 indicators that will be the final success or failure test of the programmes. All the efforts of the quality programme should point to these indicators. Use the most appropriate data collection, graphic and display techniques to measure reality and portray it to everyone. Discuss progress, success and failure in terms of the agreed indicators.

Rewards and incentives. Human beings will do something for only so long without getting some form of tangible or intrinsic reward. Money, recognition, responsibility, photographs, plaques and even red ribbons can be powerful incentives. Go for a combination of tangibles and intangibles along with extrinsic and intrinsic rewards. People respond to treats, money in the bank and compliments in the file. Each of us wants something different based on our current needs, so this part of the plan must have variety and frequent updates. The test is whether or not the reward leads to continued good performance.

Rate your quality programme

Tick the boxes that apply to rate your quality programme.

Exists	Up to date	Effective	
☐	☐	☐	Overall plan
☐	☐	☐	Commitment and support
☐	☐	☐	Education and training
☐	☐	☐	Tools and materials
☐	☐	☐	Total participation
☐	☐	☐	Measurement indicators
☐	☐	☐	Rewards and incentives

9. How to support your quality programme

A quality programme needs a lot of support from management and employees to ensure success.

Everyone wants to do a quality job. However, a formal quality programme takes time and energy. It also requires visible and verbal dedication from everyone involved. For some people this demand seems unnecessary. In reality, for a quality programme to flourish, it must have enthusiastic, ongoing support from management and employees. Each group must make a noise about quality. Lots of noise! Here are two exercises, one for managers and one for employees, to suggest positive ways of showing support for your organisation's quality programme. When you have completed your assessments, share your lists and ask for suggestions from other people to reinforce your commitment to your quality goals.

Cornerstone of quality 3

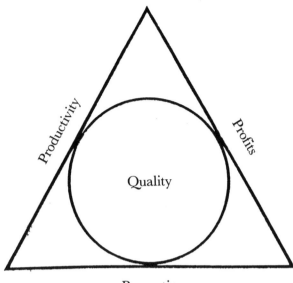

How management and employees can show support

1. How management can show support

Some managers feel pressure because they *are* supporting quality. Others are beginning new quality programmes and would like more guidelines. Still others need a shot in the arm. Listed below are eight suggestions for showing your support. Read them and tick those you are already doing and any you have decided to do. In the space below, list other support actions you have taken, and those you will begin.

Support for quality.

Already doing	Will do	
☐	☐	1. Give out pertinent quality information on strategy, goals, customers and finances.
☐	☐	2. Visibly attend presentations, conferences, individual sessions and staff meetings.
☐	☐	3. Solicit ideas and suggestions for changes that will benefit customers.

☐ ☐ 4. Attend training meetings.

☐ ☐ 5. Make training available to all employees.

☐ ☐ 6. Understand and support the system for measuring PS.

☐ ☐ 7. Understand and support the reward system. (This assumes one exists!)

☐ ☐ 8. Show visible and verbal acceptance of our quality programme.

This is what else I'm doing: This is what else I intend to do:

_____   _____

_____   _____

2. How employees can show support

Managers are often criticised for their lack of support for quality programmes. They will be more effective in their efforts when they have positive support from their employees. Here are some things you can do to support your manager, the programme and your colleagues. Listed below are six suggestions for showing your support. Read them and tick those you are already doing and those you have decided to do. In the space below, list other support actions you have taken, then list others you wish to begin.

Already   Will
doing   do

☐ ☐ 1. Learn and perform all aspects of my job well.

☐ ☐ 2. Question decisions that lower quality.

☐ ☐ 3. Set good performance examples for colleagues.

☐ ☐ 4. Establish and follow a Seven-Step Plan.

☐ ☐ 5. Attend training that is offered.

☐ ☐ 6. Apply principles and techniques from training or books to the job.

This is what else I'm doing: This is what else I intend to do:

_____   _____

_____   _____

10. How to make quality work

High motivation
Objective listening
Workable goals

Timely training
Obtainable standards

Meaningful measurements
Attention to causes
Keen spirit
Error prevention

Quick detection
Unwavering commitment
Agreement
Lifelong process
Integrity
Teamwork
Yes we can attitude

Wise leadership
Observable results
Recognition of achievement
Knowledge

◄ CHAPTER 7 ►

A MENTION OF PREVENTION

'The error that does not exist cannot be missed.'

Philip Crosby

Prevention implies that problems can be resolved before they occur. In other words, an organisation's goals should be to do the job right the first time. If an engineering company wants to build a bridge, it creates blueprints that meet structural specifications. Imagine pouring concrete and laying beams on both sides of a river and *hoping* they will meet in the middle when the bridge is complete.

Anticipating and preventing errors is less expensive than correcting them.

Correcting a problem after it has occurred is always more expensive and frustrating than anticipating errors and taking preventive action. The secret of error prevention is knowing your process. Are you making semiconductors? Hamburgers? Deals? Where are the problems likely to occur? List them. Check them.

Implement Statistical Quality Control whereby each variable of a process is identified and measured.

In manufacturing, this checking process is called *statistical quality control* (SQC). Each variable of a process is identified and measured. If it moves out of control, it is readjusted. The trick is to keep all the variables within tolerance levels. SQC shouldn't be a problem. People who make the control charts must be skilled, but people viewing them need to master only a few key items. Employees run into problems with SQC because the process isn't very exciting, and some people feel it interferes with their resourcefulness. Managers and supervisors get caught in the hero trap – unless a process is rescued at the brink of disaster, there isn't enough trouble to worry about ... and no personal recognition.

For this reason, prevention isn't a particularly popular concept. It has been described as:

- Uninteresting
- Unexciting
- Unrewarding
- Unentertaining
- Uneventful.

Workers don't get big gold medals for prevention, because they don't do anything visible or heroic. Managers of quality departments are seldom headliners in the company newsletter. They are the quiet people behind the scenes who are committed to slaying phantom dragons before they materialise. They are doing the silent job of making things work right and show up on schedule.

Principles of prevention

In a well-conceived quality programme, prevention is a primary focus. Even though it may be difficult to sell, it is the backbone of all successful quality programmes. Prevention cuts waste, saves money and increases productivity. Here is a list describing principles of prevention. Put a 'T' for true next to those you think are true, and an 'F' next to those you think are false. See the answers at the end of the list.

Prevention is the main aim: it cuts waste, saves money, increases productivity.

True   False

_____ _____   1. Prevention means doing the job right the first time.

_____ _____   2. Quality is best ensured through inspection.

_____ _____   3. A positive attitude, communication and teamwork are all vital elements of prevention.

_____ _____   4. The simpler the plan or design, the less chance there is of error.

_____ _____   5. Prevention is solely the responsibility of the chief inspection engineer.

_____ _____   6. People improve their 'prevention attention' with incentives and training.

—— —— 7. Written requirements eliminate the need for prevention.

—— —— 8. Mistakes happen because people don't regard prevention as important.

—— —— 9. Prevention is easier when you understand your job completely.

—— —— 10. Prevention is more important in manufacturing than in a service business.

Answers. 1. T; 2. F (Quality is best ensured through prevention. Inspection is expensive and creates a watchdog attitude.) 3.–4. T; 5. F (Prevention is everyone's responsibility. The more people involved, the more likely that problems will be discovered quickly.) 6. T; 7. F (Written requirements help you to understand the process and goals; they do not eliminate problems.) 8.–9. T; 10. F (Prevention is equally important in both areas, but approaches to prevention may differ.)

How to prevent errors

Prevention is based on the following:

1. Clearly understanding the requirements
2. Taking the requirements seriously
3. Vigilance
4. Understanding all the functions of your job or process *intimately*
5. Doing your job right the first time
6. Working towards continual improvement
7. Common sense (it is still in fashion).

The young accountant in the following story could take heed of the principles listed above.

James is a new accountant in a large Manchester accounting firm. He became frustrated when his columns of numbers would not tally correctly. Finally, in desperation, he added this line to the bottom of his data sheet: ESU £112.18. When his manager asked what the ESU meant, James reluctantly explained, 'Error Somewhere Unknown.'

The true cost of defective work or mediocre service is almost impossible to measure. It will always be less costly to prevent mistakes than to scramble, scrap and straighten, because scrambling occurs after the fact. Quality is not achieved through inspection and testing only – these are expensive, time-consuming methods. Reality and common sense still indicate that the best system for ensuring consistent quality is steadfastly to promote prevention as a clear priority.

Bad work costs money. Prevention is cheaper than correction.

Prevention v Correction

The 10–1 Pay-off

Prevention is ... spending time recording a message completely and fully so that you or someone else can respond properly.
— while **correction is** spending ten (10) times as many *minutes* to decipher, call back and double check the meaning of the original message.

Prevention is ... stopping the car and looking at a map to get an accurate and direct route to a city centre address.
— while **correction is** spending ten (10) times as much petrol driving down one-way streets, getting parking tickets and scaring pedestrians.

Prevention is ... providing good training and describing broad departmental goals so that every employee can see exactly how his or her work fits in and contributes.
— while **correction is** spending ten (10) times as many *hours* reprimanding, re-training, and doing the work yourself.

Prevention is ... spending one month learning the correct way to install and operate the office personal computer for word processing, database management and spreadsheets.
— while **correction is** spending ten (10) times as many *months* re-installing software, losing data and going back to the 'old' way of doing things.

Prevention is ... asking the right questions and taking the time to dig out the 'root' of the morale problems once and for all.
— while **correction is** spending ten (10) times as many *hours/pounds* trying half-baked solutions that deepen the feelings of mistrust and frustration.

◀ CHAPTER 8 ▶

QUALITY BEGINNING TO END: A REVIEW

Summary

Chapter 1. Quality Consciousness
- Quality is a goal or a set of requirements.
- Quality consciousness is the first step in implementing a personal or organisational quality plan.
- 'No worse than anyone else' is not a quality philosophy.
- Quality standards have many advantages and few disadvantages.

Chapter 2. Personal Quality Standards
- Personal quality standards control our actions and decisions all day, every day.
- Setting goals improves personal quality standards.
- Individuals make hundreds of quality decisions every day.
- Any time you expect products, services or activities to meet certain standards use your Q-MATCH (Meets Agreed Terms and CHanges) to assess your results.
- Quality is meeting expectations. Set useful workable standards with your P-A-S Options. Use Perfect, Average or Stretch depending on your goals.
- We compromise our quality standards for the following reasons: need for approval, fear of failure (or success), convenience, time, overwhelming obstacles and fatigue.

Chapter 3. The Three Cs of Quality
- Commitment, competence and communication are the cornerstones of quality.

- Commitment is a decisive personal or organisational choice to *follow through* on an agreed plan of action.
- Competence is know-how. Improved competence through experience and education improves quality.
- Communication is a common understanding among individuals and groups. Breakdowns occur when purposes are unclear.
- Commitment, competence and communication should be acknowledged and rewarded.

Chapter 4. Your Organisation's Goals
- Quality standards are based on your organisation's written policies and goals.
- Goals help organisations to determine what they do: solve problems, manufacture products, provide services.
- If quality goals are set from the top they must be agreed at all levels.
- Organisational agreement, education and management support ensure successful goal control.

Chapter 5. PS: The Perfection Standard
- Perfection Standard (PS) depends on the need for perfect products or services.
- PS is based on results-orientated attitudes.
- If perfection is not necessary, it should not be the goal.
- Use the Seven-Step Plan to measure your performance and quality goals for your work tasks (see page 52).
- Your PS is successful if you can show results.

The 'How-To' of Quality
- These ten basic components of quality are helpful in beginning or changing a quality programme:

  1. Identify and solve quality problems. A commitment to quality means stopping the process and solving the problem.
  2. Ensure customer satisfaction. Quality is what the customer says it is. Respect your customers and encourage their feedback.
  3. Measure results. Constantly collect data to see where you stand.
  4. Reward quality performance. Formal and informal rewards keep the romance in quality programme.
  5. Set up quality performance. Quality circles, quality councils, quality panels and rolestorming sessions provide group support and pinpoint quality problems.

6. Provide quality training. Education is the beginning and end of all quality programmes.
7. Assess the cost of quality. Costs are prevention costs, appraisal costs and failure costs. Costs go up as prevention goes down.
8. Establish your quality programme. To establish a quality programme you need a plan, commitment, education, tools, participation, support, measurement and rewards.
9. Support your quality programme. Quality programmes take time, energy and support from both management and employees.
10. How to make quality work from motivation and training, to attitude and leadership, all together spelling quality and success.

Chapter 7. A Mention of Prevention

- Prevention implies that problems can be resolved by anticipating them before they occur.
- Correcting problems after they occur is more expensive than anticipating errors and taking preventive action.
- To prevent errors, know your process or service.
- Prevention is unpopular because it is uninteresting.
- Common sense promotes prevention.
- Prevention v correction is a 10–1 pay-off.

◀ GLOSSARY ▶

Acceptable Quality Level (AQL). Predetermined levels of defects that will be accepted.

Appraisal. The inspection of the results of performance (product, service or activity) after it has been started or completed.

Baseline Data. Performance measurement taken before trying a new method or technique.

Commitment. The motivation and desire to continue acting on beliefs, opinions and responsibilities.

Communication. The process of sending a message through selected channels to a receiver and then getting feedback to check for mutual understanding.

Competence. The self-assurance of knowing how to do something well. It is based on education and experience.

Conformity to specification. Formal definition for quality.

Corrective action. The process of correcting problems when the preventive approach is not used or does not work. This is the most expensive way to remedy problem situations.

Cost of conformity. Cost of ensuring that things are done right. Includes prevention and appraisal.

Cost of non-conformity. The cost of doing things wrong. Includes internal and external failures.

Cost of quality. Cost of conformity + cost of non-conformity.

Customers. Those inside and outside an organisation who depend on the output of your efforts. They receive the work that you complete.

Error Cause Removal (ECR). A programme where employees list problems interfering with good quality performance. Management then assigns the appropriate group or person to solve the problem.

Failure. Internal failures are problems (non-conformity) found before going to the customer. External failures are found at the client's location or in the field.

Goals. Specific milestones or objectives that you, your department or your organisation wish to accomplish.

Management. Getting results through people by planning, organising, directing, staffing and controlling.

Measurement. A record of past performance used to influence future performance. Usually in the form of quantity, quality, cost, time or accuracy.

Non-conformity. Not meeting the specified requirements.

Organisational goals. Stated, written or implied levels of accomplishment by groups of people with common aims.

P-A-S Options. Three levels of standards (Perfection, Average, Stretch) used to gear performance to the appropriate level of customer expectations.

Perfection Standard. (Seven-Step Programme) Measures used to see if performance matches customer requirements.

Personal Quality Standards. Quality measures for personal life based on values, opinions and individual goals.

Planning. Outlining necessary requirements beforehand for the accomplishment of goals. Part of the preventive approach to quality.

PONC. Price of non-conformity. What it costs when you don't meet customer expectations.

Prevention. Anticipating and eliminating potential errors before they occur.

Preventive approach. Avoiding problems before they occur leads to better products and services at lower costs.

Productivity. The ratio between *inputs* (labour, time, capital, energy) and the end product or *outputs* (widgets, services, completed product). Productivity can be increased either by reducing the input or increasing the output.

Quality. Conformity to specifications or requirements. Quality *does not* mean the 'goodness' of a product, your job or a service.

Quality awareness. The general awareness of quality principles and their effects on the organisation.

Quality control. The process of ensuring the conformity to the designated requirements of a product or service. Often referred to as a department.

Quality education. Knowledge, skills and practice aimed at preventing, recognising and correcting poor quality performance.

Quality groups. Usually made up of teams of 6 to 12 people from an organisation who study and apply quality improvement principles to work problems.

Q-MATCH. The acid test for professional and personal quality. *Quality = Meets Agreed Terms and CHanges.*

Requirements. All attributes, utilities, features and benefits the customer expects to receive with the product or service. Your customer may be your boss, a colleague or another department.

Rework. Doing something at least one extra time because of non-conformity to requirements.

Statistical quality control. The use of statistical techniques for active control during the process. Makes use of real-time data for decision making. Also called *statistical process control* (SPC).

Trend chart. Historical data shown in a graphic format. Usually in the form of line or bar graphs.

Zero defects. The idea that perfection is the goal and no defects should be tolerated.

◀ BIBLIOGRAPHY ▶

Philip Crosby *Quality Without Tears*, McGraw-Hill, 1984
Bert Decker *How to Communicate Effectively*, Kogan Page, 1989
Twyla Dell *How to Motivate People*, Kogan Page, 1989
Thomas Gilbert *Human Competence*, McGraw-Hill, 1978
Malcolm Peel *Customer Service*, Kogan Page, 1987
Thomas Peters and Nancy Austin, *Passion for Excellence*, Collins, 1985

Further reading from Kogan Page

Effective Meeting Skills, Marion E Haynes
Effective Performance Appraisals, Robert B Maddux
Effective Presentation Skills, Steve Mandel
The Fifty-Minute Supervisor, Elwood N Chapman
How to Develop a Positive Attitude, Elwood N Chapman
How to Develop Assertiveness, Sam R Lloyd
Make Every Minute Count, Marion E Haynes
Managing Disagreement Constructively, Herbert S Kindler
Sales Training Basics, Elwood N Chapman
Successful Negotiation, Robert B Maddux
Team Building, Robert B Maddux
Ten Keys to Dynamic Customer Relations, Gregory H Sorensen